The Camper's Guide to Outrunning the Grim Reaper: A Grumpy Woman's Perspective

Pat Kanis

ISBN: 1535148802
ISBN 13: 9781535148801

Dedicated to my daughters Cassie and Laura,

and

to my truly genuine husband, Tom,
without whom I would have nothing to write about.

Disclaimer

This book is a loose description based on the author's experiences, observations, reflections, and opinions. Any similarities otherwise are purely coincidental. In some situations, exact names and locations have been changed to protect the privacy of others, or because I was too lazy to do the research.

In addition, the author holds no responsibility for grammar, spelling, or punctuations errors, as one can only review and edit so many times before insanity sets in.

You've got the red pen.....have at it!

Contents

1

How Did I Get Here?

Let me make it perfectly clear that camping was never a high priority on my bucket list. I kept no personal reminder to buy "used camper in like-new condition, pots and pans included." No topographic map of America thumbtacked to my dining room wall.. No last will and testament directing my husband to sprinkle my remains throughout a mosquito-infested forest somewhere in the Cascade Mountains. Of course, I love nature and the outdoors just like any warm-blooded American citizen living west of the great divide...a hike here, a bike ride there. And what baby boomer didn't have a childhood that included a good camp in the pristine wilderness, somewhere within five miles of home, spending endless summer days swimming in spring-fed lakes, roasting hot dogs over an open fire, and not showering for an entire week?

The important question is what reasonably sane, sixty-year-old woman truly lusts for her golden years on the road less traveled in an RV?

Did I really just reveal that I'm sixty? My friend Kathryn, who had always gone by the name "Kathy" until she went through her midlife crisis and decided that she preferred to be called "Kathryn," even though I tried to tell her that nearly every tragic female literary figure in history was named Kathryn, once told me that turning sixty was horrible. "There's *nothing* young about sixty...unless you die; then everyone says, 'Oh, she was so young, just sixty.'"

We've all seen them. White-head Q-tips, heading down the interstates in their seventy-plus-foot retirement homes with childhood dreams attached—bikes, canoes, and fishing paraphernalia along with a cute little Honda CRV and lap dog named Buster. Frankly, I trusted those bumper stickers that specified that they were simply spending their children's inheritance. I never thought that they might have a true wanderlust for driving about the country until their hemorrhoids cried "uncle." I honestly figured that their ungrateful, self-centered children were pushing them to insanity and that they, the parents, had decided to pull up stakes and make a run for it before the dearies had even noticed that they, and the money, were gone.

So you can imagine my mild bewilderment when one day in early September my husband, Tom, announced that after researching makes and models, he had found us the perfect travel trailer. "It looks real nice in the picture here. See, honey?" He showed me photos of a twenty-three-footer posted on Craigslist and read aloud the explanatory comments.

"It says original owner. I can see that it's been well cared for."

Indeed, it was a very pretty unit and appeared to be in perfect condition, but where was this going? I began to sweat like I used to do in elementary school whenever Sister Ann Elizabeth walked past my desk.

My husband wasted no time in taking me with him to check it out. Nor did he waste any time in completing the transaction. He was as excited as a seven-year-old at the sight of his first bicycle on Christmas day. Well, Christmas Day several decades ago. I don't think a bike would qualify for excitement these days, given the true ecstasy found in electronic options.

Here's the thing. I'm not sure what made Tom think that camping was on my pleasure inventory. I'm sort of an "uptown girl" and a rather prissy one at that, if you know what I mean—beachfront condo, suntan lotion, and metallic string bikini—ha-ha...gotcha on that last one. But I admit that I may have presented myself quite differently when I first met him.

It was one of those midlife things, I tell you. Both of my daughters had successfully blossomed into adulthood, and a recent, yet civil, end to my twenty-six-year marriage offered me choices and opportunities that I had never paused to consider before. I'd say "paths," but I just hate when people start talking about "paths." I'm on this path...we all choose our own paths, blah, blah, blah. It's right up there with "journey." Enjoy the journey...learn from the journey...don't forget to include the Imodium-AD on your journey. Yeah, life is just one big backpacking trip to Kathmandu.

Anyway, initially I chose the direction of many middle-age women. I changed my eating habits and lost weight. I colored the gray, shortened the skirts, and heightened the heels. I began to exercise daily: step aerobics, jogging, biking, and dance classes. I joined the Mountaineers, a hiking club, which coincidentally had an over-fifty group, and it was at a Mountaineers-sponsored dance that I first met Tom.

Well, he was not seventeen, if you know what I mean, but the way he danced...truly, the man could slow dance a woman's legs into Jell-O. He told me that his mother had made him take dancing lessons when he was in the sixth grade, thus the skill for turning women into Jell-O.

Tom, a widower with three grown children, was of medium build, mildly bald, sporting a gray moustache and a heart-warming smile. He also had a friendly, easy gift of gab. As we danced, he told me about his late wife and the cancer that had taken her life. When I asked him where he lived and what had brought him so far from home to this dance, he replied, "Because it's been two months since anyone has crossed my doorstep, and I couldn't bear to stay one more night at home alone."

That was enough for me. I was a goner, smitten, besotted, hooked. Tom and I soon became fast friends. We hiked together, danced together, traveled together, and slept together. Well, OK, so we were "sleepover" kinds of friends. It was nice. Definitely nice.

Tom and his family own a very rustic cabin in the mountains, and one weekend Tom invited me to join him for one such sleepover, with a little hiking on the side. The cabin sat on the banks of the most beautiful creek I had ever seen, with dozens of sparkling white waterfalls and an amazing canopy of trees. Situated in the thick of the forest, the cabin was rather dark but cozy inside with ceramic squirrels, often minus an appendage or two—created by some great relative down the ancestral line—adorning the log walls, along with a collection of cast-iron trivets and wads of old newspaper shoved into the cracks, for whatever reason. It was furnished with a couple of old sofas, a picnic table, a wood-burning stove for heat, and another for cooking.

The cabin had electricity but no running water. All potable water needed to be brought in jugs from home, and water for all other uses—that is, washing hands and faces, washing dishes, and so forth—was hauled up from the creek and kept in buckets on the porch.

Do you sense where this is leading? No bathroom. No shower. Just a two-seated outhouse back behind the woodshed. Now, I'm no weenie—well, actually, I am, but I considered myself reasonably capable of roughing it as well as the next gal. I could get by one day with a spit bath. I could substitute brushing my teeth with chewing gum for a while. Heck, it could even be sort of fun bringing in wood from the shed, hauling water up the bank from the creek, and cooking griddle cakes (most ordinary people call them pancakes, but we wilderness survivors refer to them as griddle cakes) on the wood-burning stove. And then sleeping in the loft all snug in a two-hundred-pound sleeping bag, just my newly found love and me...and whatever insect or rodent happened to wander in to join us, which was always the case.

Except for those last two items, I could say that the day of my first cabin sleepover was probably one of the happiest days of my life, right up there with the carnival that a next-door neighbor from my childhood put on one sunny summer day in her backyard when I was about six years old.

I grew up in Akron, Ohio, in an area called Goodyear Heights. It was a marvelous place for kids to grow up in the '50s.

Cathy's backyard carnival offered lots of games and prizes, and I had come home with the best prize ever—a change purse. Now, I don't remember what the change purse looked like, nor do I remember exactly how I had won it, but I do remember sitting on the john later that day declaring to myself that this was the happiest day of my life. So it must have been true.

Anyway, back to the cabin. Sooner or later, as any person of middle age or older will attest, nature will and does call in the middle of the night. Midnight. Two o'clock in the morning. No time is sacred. When you have to go, you have to go. And in this scenario, the only place to go is down the loft ladder, out the front door, off the porch to the right, down a dark, unnerving path that veers behind the woodshed until a couple of just-below-the-surface tree roots send you tripping head-on into the outhouse door.

First, be advised that there is a padlock on this door so that hikers, mountain bikers, and other strangers don't perceive this as a free-to-the-public facility and use up all your toilet paper, a very big sacrilege, and thus leaving you to search for leaves or pine needles.

Second, once you have freed the lock and entered the dark, eerie domain, do not, I repeat, *do not* look around. It would be better if you did not know the color, size, or location of the regional jungle arachnids. Just do what you've got to do, lock up, and get the hell out of there.

I almost forgot to tell you, though, to keep in mind that this mountain forest is home to the following: squirrels (no big deal), rabbits (ho hum), elk (may startle you by their size), coyotes (give me the creeps), cougars, and bears, oh my!

Yeah, now let's see how fast you run! And don't forget that the forests of the great Northwest are also known to be home to Sasquatch.

No, I'm serious. It's true. You might have read about Sasquatch or seen a blurred, mystifying photo of him in a magazine somewhere, running through some undisclosed dark forest. They do exist.

I actually dated a Sasquatch in college in the early '70s. Back then, he masqueraded as a college fraternity brother going by the name of Jay. A bushy fellow. Arrogant, sarcastic, and temperamental. Jewish, I believe.

5

I disengaged myself from the prehistoric beast after a single date, sensing the vast difference in our gene pools. Last I saw of Sasquatch Jay was in the university cafeteria with his blond sorority-sister girlfriend, following two obligatory paces behind him. So sad to witness how the genes mutate. Ouch!

My yoga instructor says that they are called "monkey thoughts." Like monkeys that swing from limb to limb in a tree, so do the thoughts of people like me. My sisters suggest that I have ADD, because I never finish one sentence of a conversation before moving on to another thought. It could be a sign of genius, though.

So given the several long weekends at Tom's cabin (forget about the "uncle" thing, because he has already heard it), as well as two or three tent-camping trips down the coast of Oregon and California, I can see where I may have somehow given Tom the impression that I was someone who preferred to cast all modern conveniences aside for the primitive ways of our ancestors. Tom was aware, however, that I did not and would not ever backpack into the bowels of the vast yonder with him. In the course of some previous polite discussion, I had explained to him that, although I did enjoy a bit of nature hiking, I refused to haul my bed and breakfast along with me.

Nevertheless, I was a willing player in the game of pitch-the-tent for a while. Along the Oregon coast, we once spent a weekend camped across from a sand dune romantically devoting our evenings to watching the sunset behind the pink oceanic horizon. Frankly, that's where romance drew its Harlequin line. There were meals to make, dishes to wash, and showers to take, all in the most primordial fashion.

It was attending to personal hygiene that I found most challenging on these trips. In general, when you contemplate bathing, you check out the facilities in advance. Commonly consisting of one or two showers and one or two toilets (side note: taking a shower next to a person attending to her "daily constitutional" is not a pleasant experience), the condition of most bathrooms could be rated from "It'll do" to "No way!" Additionally, in many parks, the showers are often unisex and, depending on which campground, appear to be cleaned only about once every year or two.

Generally, there is a steady line of equally hygiene-deficient campers, which requires you to stand in the queue with towel, toiletries, and clean clothes in hand for up to an hour waiting for your turn. Once you are inside, there is all this pressure to quickly disrobe, deposit your quarters, shower at the speed of lightning, and redress so as not to hold up the line of other tired, stinky outdoor vacationers.

On one particular trip, we traveled to the redwoods of California, and by the time we had arrived at our selected campground, being the genius that I was, I had pretty much plotted out my showering strategy. It was a brilliant strategy, really. Rather than stand in an endless line of weary tent dwellers who were miserably waiting and dreaming of their warm moment of rapture, I would postpone my shower until later—much later, like eleven o'clock. Then I would have the whole place to myself. No rushing to appease the impatient mob. No grunting neighbor in the next stall—just me, hot water, and solitude.

And so, at my prearranged time and barely able to keep my eyes open, I gathered up my washcloth, towel, soap, shampoo, shaving cream, razor, hair dryer, and brush, plus enough quarters to indulge in complete bliss for at least ten minutes. I headed off to the shower, and just as I had expected, I had the whole place to myself. Yes!

Carefully, not wanting to waste a single precious minute of warm water on the details of tool location, I placed my towel and clean clothes on the bench, far enough away to stay dry, and then lined up all of my toiletries within arm's reach. I removed my dirty clothes and placed my glasses in a safe place close enough to reach in case I ran into difficulty reading hot versus cold.

When I was finally ready, I took my quarters in hand and put the first one in the money slot. It slid down. Halfway down. Then it stopped. What the...

I pushed the return coin button. Nothing. I repeated the urgently-want-my-quarter-back tactic at least ten additional times until I finally came to the near-hysterical realization that the quarter machine was jammed. No deposits. No returns. No freakin' shower.

But wait. I remembered that in that particular structure, there were not one but two showers. With near frantic desperation, I grabbed it all...toiletries, washcloth and towel, dirty clothes, and hair dryer, and flew buck naked out of stall number one into the safety of stall number two. Step one of escape to hygienic well-being successfully executed.

Maintaining my uptown girl composure, I threw everything into a single large pile on the floor, and with the steady hand of a bank robber about to open the vault, I dropped one quarter into the slot. Ping. I held my eye-to-coin-slot contact and inserted another quarter. Ping. Praise the Lord! I was up to four minutes of cautiously anticipated rapture. Third quarter in, I slid my finger over to the "On" button and pushed it. Houston, we have liftoff. It's water! Warm water! My very own warm water! Hard fought and honestly won. It was a proud moment.

How mindboggling the speed at which pleasurable time flies, those six minutes of warm water bliss. It didn't matter. In the blink of a gnat's eye, I felt amazingly released of all of nature's residue. After towel drying and putting on clean sweats for a good night's sleep, I gathered up all my belongings, shoved them into a plastic bag, and stepped out of the stall to comb and dry my hair.

I laid my bag down on the counter by the sinks and looked around for an electrical outlet for my hairdryer. Uh-oh. I looked to the left. I looked to the right. I looked above the sinks, under the sinks, and all across the bathroom. Nothing. Eleven thirty-five at night, wet hair, and no outlet. I sighed with the defeat of a child who had just chased the Jingle Joe truck six blocks only to be told that they were all sold out of popsicles.

I contemplated throwing myself down on the floor and having a temper tantrum, but I figured it wouldn't help anything anyway. Besides, who knew *what* was on those floors.

Just then, two young girls, who looked to be about seventeen years old or so, walked in. They seemed surprised to see me there and stood a moment gawking.

"There doesn't appear to be an electrical outlet in here for me to dry my hair." I smiled weakly, my powerless hair dryer still in hand. I had expected a tad bit of sympathy, or better, directions to the location of an available plug. What I got instead was what could only be defined as an incredibly profound California Valley Girl perspective of the situation.

"*Duh*," they sang in unison. "It's called camping."

The two nymphets laughed hysterically and proceeded to execute one of those "high five" things, thoroughly entertained by their sheer cleverness. One would have guessed that they had chosen door number three, resulting in the winning of an Easy Bake Oven or something equally impressive for the IQ of the duo before me.

My first impulse was to slap both of the snots silly. But the wisdom of my years along with a strong sense of self-preservation—I was pretty sure I could not outrun them—pressed me to don my oh-so-luminous halo, which I save for just such occasions, gather up my belongings, and haul my freshly showered, middle-aged butt back to the tent.

Tom greeted me with a warm hug and genuine sympathy. But knowing the man as I did, I sensed that he was chuckling to himself.

In the end, we sat in the dark, starry night next to a warm fire waiting for my hair to dry, not saying a word, just holding hands and happy to be where we were—together. Life is good.

2

Iraqi Cat

When it comes to summer travel, I have learned three things to be true: 1) the Spanish sentiment "mi casa es su casa" loses its sincerity in the English translation; 2) rabid pets are the norm in most households; and 3) the blissful excitement of summer vacation stops the minute you cross the Continental Divide.

It took two full days to journey from Washington to Idaho, morphing from wearing double-layered sweatshirts to "barely there" tanks. After one vapor lock, one beer-bottle landslide, two soft-soap eruptions, three "beware of rattlesnakes" warnings, and a total meltdown of all chocolate on board, we arrived at Tom's sister's house, travel trailer waving with excited anticipation.

To our dismay, neither Tom's sister nor her husband were home from work yet, so we peeled our sweaty thighs from the seats of the pickup and got out to survey the neighborhood. The temperature was in the nineties and a tad oppressive for rainforest dwellers. But not to worry, we were on vacation! It wasn't long before a next-door neighbor spotted us and meandered over for a chat. Tom, ever the social gabber, was in his element.

Her name was Teresa, a single homeowner and cute as a button. But don't let the image of all that wholesomeness reel you in, as in the course of a few short minutes, she managed to divulge a story, a vision of such nightmarish proportions that it left us greatly unnerved and drenched in a smoldering anxiety for the remainder of our stay. OK, it left *me* rattled. Tom didn't seem the least bit fazed. Keep in mind that Tom's thoughts tend to be perpetually focused on *I wonder what's for dinner.*

Anyhow, it so happened that one dark, rainy night—I employ meteorological and literary liberties here—Teresa came home from work to find her two little schnauzers in a highly agitated state. Not only were they hiding in the laundry room but they were also emitting sounds that were something between hesitant barks and foreboding whimpers.

Teresa sensed that someone or something was in the house, so seizing her purse—that's right, the ever so terror-evoking purse—began her dreaded but necessary search through the house, turning on the lights to each room as she advanced, dogs at her heels.

When she closed in on her bedroom, the two dogs' agitation heightened, and they began to take on a vicious stance never before attempted, at least by them. Their growls and gazes pointed Teresa to the space beneath her bed, and with considerable caution, she lowered herself to her hands and knees and lifted the bed skirt. And there it was. The beast! A nightmarish hallucination! Terror incarnate! It was...the Iraqi Cat!

As the story goes, a few months back, Tom's sister decided to adopt a new cat. It seems that the one dog and two cats she already possessed were not sufficient for her benevolent household. His sister is a woman with a very loving, generous heart, and such love and generosity reached all the way to the doors of the city's animal shelter. Who knows what twist of fate lead her to become the new caregiver, not master, of a freshly immigrated cat from Iraq.

Two-foot-long legs, a foot-long body, and thirty pounds of white fur, she was simply known by all as the "Iraqi Cat." This cat, skittish for obvious reasons, did not take kindly to forward gestures—as in, *do not touch!* If I want you, I'll let you know. Otherwise, don't even look at me.

Teresa knew about the cat, had even seen it once or twice, and now guessed that it had somehow finagled its way into her house through her doggie door sometime during the day.

She knew that there was only one way out for the cat, and she also knew that she would have to assist it. After taking her dogs and locking them up in the laundry room, she proceeded to open every door and window to the outside. With harried trepidation, she returned to her bedroom, stooped down, spotted the crouched cat, and reached.

Wrong move, not to mention incredibly naive. The cat, which had become enraged by what she perceived as two parts of a dangerous and menacing enemy coming toward her, immediately latched on. And Teresa, reacting to the painfully executed latching, wasted no time in retracting her arms from beneath the bed. Unfortunately, the cat elected to arrive right along with her arms, still attached...teeth, claws—the works.

The young woman's highly developed instinct of self-preservation advised her to shake the crazed feline off, but her equally developed rational self at the same time commanded her to remain as still as the grave. Eventually, the hysterical cat released itself from Teresa's bleeding arms and bolted down the hall.

By some unwitnessed miracle, the cat found its frenzied way out of the house while Teresa called 9-1-1. One trip to the ER and several shots later, she is still the talk of the neighborhood. So is the Iraqi Cat. As a fellow pet owner, Teresa proved admirably understanding, but my guess is that the doggie door now sports a few dozen nails.

Now comes my dilemma. I've never particularly cared for cats. I'm just not a "cat" person. You know, you're either a "cat person" or a "dog person" or neither. I am neither, although I am tolerant of dogs with which I am familiar and vice versa. And the dog must be kind and gentle, not beastly or hyper.

But cats and I just don't jive. I don't know why. You've heard of "white coat syndrome" as a cause of elevated blood pressure while in the doctor's office? Mine would be called "tabby terror" at the sight of a cat. And as everyone will tell you, cats always know which person in the room is the cat lover and which person is not. Cats will zero in on the nonlover and engage in the same game that they enjoy playing with mice. You can't fool them, no siree. I've experienced cats that have climbed up me or who have jumped onto my lap and dug their claws in ("Oh, that's just what cats do.") They have hissed at me, bitten my legs and feet, or simply sat on the floor staring at me, knowing very well that their glaring eyes were making me a nervous wreck.

I have nightmares about cats biting me, unable to shake them off. What do you think this means? I'm sweating like a whore in church right now just writing about it.

So what was I to do now? We were at Tom's sister's house with plans to stay for two days, and I was in an unreasonably petrified state.

After we had finished our little chat with the neighbor, Tom moseyed over to the camper to get himself a beer, so I moved to the porch to get out of the hot sun and wait for our hosts. And naturally, I no sooner sat down when, out of the corner of my eye, I detected something moving right there on the table next to me. You guessed it. The Iraqi Cat.

I knew perfectly well that I was being irrational, not to mention childish, and so I hid my anxiety as best I could. I kept half an eye on the cat for the next two days and, obviously, I lived to tell about it.

Now, where did I put my blood pressure cuff?

P.S. The cat's real name is Brooke.

3

Steps for All Ages

I'm not certain of the exact day or time that I became Queen of Wimps, but I would be the first to admit that this particular royal throne definitely fits me well and that I have firmly planted my royal butt on it. Storms, earthquakes, floods—you name it—anything with the remotest potential of danger makes me nervous, and I avoid it like the plague, which coincidentally also makes me nervous.

In my defense, I might add that I have made many valiant attempts throughout my life at being adventurous, sometimes even taking stabs at daring, risky—and once or twice, perilous—OK, perhaps not perilous, but definitely risky behavior. A toboggan ride with six other people onboard is rather daring, don't you think? And there's that snipe hunt when I was eleven. Scratch the snipe hunt. That wasn't me. That was my sister, Marcia.

Anyway, one would think that by the time one reaches middle age and notices that the hourglass of time is not even a quarter full, all caution and hesitation would be cast off like an old tin bucket of hardened concrete and that an itinerary full of fun, adventure, and novelty would begin!

Not.

Exotic travels? You never know what deadly disease you might catch.

Hot air balloon rides? Haven't you been watching the news? Some incendiary incident...I think it was somewhere in the Middle East?

How about cave exploration? What? And have to cut off my right leg with a pocket knife in order to extricate myself from the boulders I'm wedged between? I don't think so!

My husband will attest to my fearful irrationality referring to my approach to driving down a snowy mountain pass.

Sleep mask on? Check.

Headphones on? Check.

Mantras ready? Check.

Even then, I have the habit of asking him every two seconds to slow down, or to inquire as to whether or not we have traction. I might add that it is Tom's habit to always reply that we do not have traction, but that it is OK, as we are moving with the flow of traffic.

Oh, that's a relief. We're all sliding down the mountain side, but at least we are all sliding in unison.

And so the age-old question: nature or nurture? I read somewhere recently that researchers at the University of Somewhere-or-Other have tracked the irksome worrywart tendency, not only to a gene, but all the way to the exact DNA marker, or something like that. So there you go. It's not my fault. I was born that way.

Or did I learn it that way?

The reason that I bring this up has its source in a laundry mat in Vernal, Utah. Tom had deemed Dinosaur National Monument in Dinosaur, Utah, as a must stop spot. Thus, we set up camp in Steinaker State Park just outside the city of Vernal, a small city of about nine thousand-plus people—but don't quote me on that figure—whose primary industry is extracting natural resources, mainly petroleum, I think.

On the second day of our stay—you can only stare at dinosaur bones so long—we went into town, Tom to purchase a few groceries and I to do laundry at the local Laundromat.

I'll be forthright here and tell you that I don't particularly care for Laundromats. In general, they seem dirty and icky, and it takes forever to do your laundry. It's also costly. Commonly, they contain a few hard plastic chairs to sit on, have a television hanging from the ceiling, a pop machine, one or two candy machines, and one machine dispensing various detergents, bleaches, and so forth, at enormously inflated prices.

Sometimes there is a live person sitting behind a counter dispensing change, or at least paid to point to the machine that does. There are rows and rows of washing machines, bigger washing machines, and biggest washing machines. Ditto for the dryers. You have to put in lots and lots of quarters to wash just one load of clothes and lot and lots of quarters to dry them.

Now, you can't just put your laundry in the machine and leave to run other errands, because someone might steal it—not the machine, your laundry. I know that this sort of thinking seems unreasonable. After all, who would want steal my size seven granny underpants and risk having to serve time for it? But you just never know.

And another thing: never, ever use the bathroom there unless you're about to wet yourself.

And so, you sit and wait...forever. The wise thing to do is to bring something to read, but that requires some forethought. I try never to have forethoughts.

On that particular day, there were a few grubby young males who came in and out and who, I'm guessing, were workers in the petroleum industry. There was also a somewhat overweight, perspiration-soaked young fellow in shorts, sleeveless undershirt, and flip-flops sorting his laundry, and a young mother who stood by the window texting while her little boy stuck his finger up the candy machine hoping to get lucky. Some things never change.

I also observed a senior couple working on a huge laundry project. They appeared to be in their late sixties, again fairly plump—it takes one to know one—and not in the best of health. I could see, in their faces and in the way they shuffled around, that they had little energy and, more than likely, were in pain. The woman used a walker. They had about seven or eight baskets full of presorted laundry, and I could only imagine the chore it had been for the silent two to haul in the mammoth loads from their car.

As there wasn't much else to do, I sat there discreetly watching them as they proceeded with their business, filling up an entire row of washing machines with the categorized clothes followed with a cup of detergent. They had a plastic bag full of quarters and progressed to depositing the necessary amount for each of the washing machines. It seemed like an awful lot of money.

I couldn't help but wonder, *Is this how it is, then? Are our golden years wrapped in pain, poverty, and scheduled laundry days?*

The fact is that I felt uncomfortable in the laundry mat and around the people in it. I don't know why.

Because I'm a pensive kind of person, I did give it some thought, though. Was it the type of people who frequented Laundromats that made me feel uneasy? Surely, I was not fearful of poor people. I grew up poor!

Raised in a Catholic household of eight kids, I know what it's like to be poor—packing peanut butter and Miracle Whip sandwiches into a paper sack, begging writing paper and pencils from classmates, and squeezing my butterball body into my sister's size two hand-me-downs. My siblings and I didn't know, at the time, that we were poor. We just went about our business like most kids—playing, tattling—you know—everyday stuff.

That's why I can now tell you—I'm diverting from my original subject—that everything I learned about life I learned in junior high school, specifically Goodyear Junior High.

Goodyear Junior High School was a hand-me-down junior high, formerly a high school, the same one that my father had attended eons before. When it became run down, as was customary, it was converted to a junior high. Too rickety for the greater academic aspirations of high schoolers, it would do just fine for the twelve- to fourteen-year-old hooligans.

Sporting old wooden floors, old wooden desks, the original blackboards, and original smells, it also had a prehistoric swimming pool, filled with cold water and topped with an inch of floating hair resulting in an out-break of alleged perpetual menstruation in the female student population.

You see, after I completed sixth grade in the then-free parochial school, my parents decided that I was ready for the switch to public school. And as it turned out, I loved junior high school! It was the end of uniforms and stress-induced spelling bees. No more daily mass, no more hygiene inspections, and no more standing up to recite or answer a question. Book covers were a thing of the past.

Also, as I later discovered, as we parochial students were generally somewhat advanced in our studies, I didn't have to crack a book for three years!

But the best thing of all about public school junior high was that there were lots and lots of kids! All kinds of kids. White kids, black kids, even Protestants! I was in social heaven. So many friends to be made, so little time. Oh, the excitement of it all!

Since Akron was the "rubber capital" of the world, the vast majority of students at Goodyear Junior High were children of factory workers. So we had that common connection—not children of millionaires but from families with enough to get by.

Everything I know about life today, I learned in junior high. I learned about sex—not firsthand of course, but information spreads—and I learned swear words, which I eagerly tried on for size. It was where I first heard the F word, which, incidentally, I never tried on for size un-til the age of fifty, when my friend, Kelly Rae, encouraged me to break free of my puritanical yoke. What the f–? I still can't say it.

I learned that males had a strong urge to duke it out and that, some-times, so did girls. I tried my best to avoid those situations.

I learned the social ins and outs regarding boyfriends and girl-friends and going steady. I learned how to dance! I learned that I would never, ever make the cheerleading squad. I learned how easy it was to make friends and to make others laugh. I also learned about the many opportunities to piss people off.

Sometimes, you even make a new friend without trying. On the third Friday of every academic month, our school's PTA sponsored a dance.

The dance was always held in the gym of Seiberling Elementary, just up the street from my house. It was a gym with superior echo capabilities, so when "Downtown," by Petula Clark, was played, our vocals resonated superbly. Oh, such joy!

I especially enjoyed the arranged circle dance, with boys assigned to the inside circle and girls facing opposite the boy on the outside. It was the one way, actually the only way for me, a virtual social nerd-ette, to have an opportunity to dance with super popular, heart melting, English Leather—drenched handsome guys. Seize the day? Pounce on it, was my motto.

One Friday, I asked my mom if I could have some friends over after the dance, and she said that I could. There were only a handful of us—four girls and three boys—and we sat around the kitchen table eating boxed Chef Boyardee pizza and drinking colas. I didn't particularly like pizza or cola, but that was common teen cuisine back then. Come to think of it, it still is.

Anyway, we talked and laughed and were, in general, silly which was par for the age. I remember one boy, named Nolan, who was especially funny and very likeable. Nolan was new to me, brought along to my house by one of the other boys, or so I thought. It wasn't until that "I'd better be getting home" time rolled around when Nolan asked to use the phone to call his mom. The other kids lived close by and had planned on just walking home together.

So when Nolan went to use the phone, I turned to the group and asked, "Who brought Nolan?" All shoulders went into shrug mode.

"I thought you invited him," my friend Mark said.

"Me? I've never met him before tonight," I replied.

I looked at my friend, Donna, who in turn focused on our friend, David. "Isn't he a friend of yours?"

He shook his head. "Nope," was the answer.

And so it was determined that Nolan was a stray. Just fell in with us somewhere between the dance and home and followed along like a friendly puppy. Later, after quizzing him, we discovered that Nolan was new to our school and that this was his first time at our dance.

PAT KANIS

The following week, I realized that I very much liked Nolan and that Nolan liked me. We went steady for three whole days before moving on to greener pastures, or should I say, other sheep in the greener pastures. Such were junior high romances. I wonder what ever happened to him.

Alas, it was in junior high school that I also eventually learned just how naive I was about life and that all was not always as groovy as I had figured. I learned about racism from the assistant principal, Mr. Hawkins, who called me into his office one morning and threatened me about socializing with students of another color. I assure you that his words were uglier than that. He also threatened me about repeating this conversation to anyone, including my parents. I was twelve years old and a good girl, which translated to frightened, so I did what I was told.

I learned about intolerance for those whose lifestyle fell outside of what was perceived as the social norm.

I learned about mortality, when my new friend Beverly's mother died and Beverly moved to Lodi to live with her aunt. I really missed her.

I learned about tragedy when a classmate's mother backed out of the driveway, accidentally running over her seven-year-old brother and killing him.

I learned that, while girls think "love," boys think "sex" and that frequently pregnancy, along with the pain and gossip, follows.

The assassinations of the Kennedy brothers and Martin Luther King Jr., racial tension, university protests, and the Vietnam War—such was the path that led me to the eventual end of innocence.

Nevertheless, I still maintain that I enjoyed some of the best times and best friends of my life in junior high.

On this day, on a plastic chair in the laundry mat in Vernal, Utah, I sat with these recollections and marveled over the many humps, bumps, and hurdles crossed and tripped over every day since.

Why is it that I always turn toward the road of safety and familiarity rather than paddling down the river of curiosity and experience? Did I really want to live the simple, safe life? Would fear be my eternal handicap?

Nature or nurture?

"Ma'am, is this your sock?" The heavy-set young man in shorts and sleeveless undershirt stood in front of me holding up one of my hiking socks.

I had been startled. "Oh yes. Thank you," I replied, giving him an appreciative but weak smile. "I would have been wondering a long time whatever happened to that other sock."

"I know how that goes." He had a genuinely friendly face. "I have an entire drawer full of single socks. I wear them anyway, you know, mismatched. No law that says I can't." We chuckled.

Then he pointed to a spot on the floor in front of one of the washing machines. "I found your sock on the floor just over there." I remember thinking how amiable he was and how relieved I was that it wasn't a pair of my grannies that he'd found on the floor or anywhere else, for that matter.

Time seemed to drag by, and it dawned on me that I probably could have washed my laundry by hand quicker than it was taking those washing machines. With an impatient sigh, I returned my nosy attention to the senior couple, who were still busy at work, and wondered how I might help. But I had a feeling that they more than likely would have declined my offer of assistance. They appeared to be a pair with a system, a life system. Nevertheless, I admit that I regret that I didn't at least ask. I'm like that...good heart, weak follow-through.

Having the highly developed alertness of a jungle cat, I eventually sensed that both of the washing machines I had employed had stopped. I sprinted toward the machines, unloaded the clothes into a basket, proceeded to roll it about looking for an available dryer when one of the young men, one whom I had taken for a petroleum worker, flew past me heading out the door. With an arm full of hastily folded clothes, he called to me, "Ma'am, there's still fifteen minutes left on that dryer over there...if you can use it."

I remembered that there was a time when I would be shocked if someone called me "ma'am," feeling that I was much too young to be addressed as such. But now there was no denying that I had indeed arrived at the respected age of maturity that warranted the title of "ma'am."

I smiled at him and called back, "I can. Thank you." He tossed me a smile and flew out the door.

That smile felt good.

Meanwhile, the little boy across the room had apparently given up on his probe of the candy machine, but it wasn't long before I saw his young mother walk over and deposit money in the machine, giving him a small handful of candy. He seemed delighted. When he looked up from the treasure in his hand, he noticed that I was watching him. I always seem to be watching somebody.

Slowly and hesitantly, he walked over to me and held out his hand. I gave him my gentlest smile, took one and only one piece of the candy, even though it was chocolate, and thanked him. He seemed pleased. It was the best chocolate I have ever had—despite the lack of washed hands.

Sometimes, you just need to lay down your memories and fears, silence your judgment of the life around you, and just be.

A quiet gift. Vernal, Utah.

4

Never Take Anything Personally

Several years ago, while driving down the back road from Deliverance (the town where I live) to the Big City (the modern city where I wished I lived) on my way to a vision-board class, by some celestial twist of fate, I happened on an alternative radio station featuring an intuitive in Seattle. The intuitive happened at the time to be taking questions from callers. I say "intuitive" rather than "psychic" because for me, the title intuitive has an ethereal, mystical ring to it, while the word psychic has more of a psycho alarm. I like "intuitive."

Ambling along, I listened to the varied questions that callers posed, ranging from career choices to vitamin advice and with answers like, "In a previous life, you came to this country on a slave ship," to "You need to ask your unborn baby to turn, and reassure him that you will keep him safe,"—you know, stuff like that. It was quite entertaining, and I thought how fun it would be to call in. So heaven only knows what got into me, I did. I never expected that my call would be picked up and screened on my second try, but it was. I immediately pulled over into a Costco parking lot. Have to be safe, you know.

When the screener, a very pleasant young man, asked me about the nature of my question for "Janet"—at least he didn't refer to her as "Dr. Janet"—I gave it a quick mulling over but knew that only one question weighed heavily on my mind.

"Over the past few years," I told him, "I have spent a lot of time and money going to the doctor for a variety of reasons. It seems like it is one thing after another after another. I would just like to know what is behind this."

I was certain that it could not have anything to do with aging or my postmenopausal status and that "Janet" would tap into my aura, or whatever, and provide me with the very wisdom that I was seeking.

While I was tickled that the young man must have thought my question very worthy, telling me that I was second in line and that Janet would be with me shortly, I started to perspire and wondered if I was being silly and should hang up. But being the said silly woman that I am, I didn't.

After about ten minutes, the soft voice of a woman came on the line and quietly greeted me.

"This is Janet. How may I help you?"

Nervously, I related my question just as I had previously to the screener.

"Well you see, Janet," I began, as though I had actually known of her prior to this call, which I hadn't, "I just seem to be going to the doctor a lot lately, for every possible reason. It's just one thing after another, after another, and..."

At that point, Janet interrupted me and said, "I am going to recommend that you read two books. The first one is *The Four Agreements* by Don Miguel Ruiz."

I was surprised. "I have that book and have read it several times," I told her. In fact, the book had been given to me several years earlier by my friend, Sandra, a middle-school math teacher, whose real strength was in working with emotionally troubled kids and who eventually opened her own counseling practice working with the emotionally troubled parents of said kids. I believe that it was she who coined the sentiment that "all parents f—k up their children." A profound philosophy.

Anyway, without skipping a beat, Janet-the-Intuitive continued. "Then I want you to memorize that book from cover to cover. The second book is *Healing Back Pain: The Mind-Body Connection* by Dr. John Sarno. I will call you in a couple of weeks to follow up with you and to see how you are doing."

And with that, she was gone.

I wasn't sure what to think, but the first thing that came to mind was that Janet really, really had to go to the bathroom, and thus, her urgent departure. But after I gave it additional thought, I just figured that she must get a lot of similar calls from middle-age hypochondriac women and had the same advice for us all. It's all in your head. It's a cry for attention. You have the hots for Dr. Darling. She, no doubt, had a few stern words for her young screener as well. What's more, she also did not follow up with me in a couple of weeks, as promised.

And so I continued on to my vision-board class, another silly idea.

Very quickly, I will tell you what the "four agreements" are, as this information will come in very handy down the line:

The First Agreement: be impeccable with your word. Basically—and this is a very abridged version—be very kind in what you say and think about others, as well as about yourself.

The Second Agreement: don't take anything personally. It's never about you. "Personal importance" is, in essence, a maximum expression of selfishness.

The Third Agreement: never make assumptions. Just ask, and avoid misunderstandings.

The Fourth Agreement: always do your best. If you simply do your best, "you will avoid self-judgment, self-abuse, and regret."

There. With all of that explained, I will tell you just how I managed to break all of those agreements within two short days in Golden, Colorado.

— ⌒ ⌒ —

After camping one night at a most beautiful, scenic campground called Steamboat Lake, we headed over the pass toward Golden to visit Tom's old army buddy, Bud, and his wife, Nancy. Bud was a retired tax accountant, quiet and sadly recently revisited with post-traumatic stress from his experience in Vietnam. Nancy was an environmentalist (please reuse your cloth napkins throughout your visit with us) working on her PhD in religious studies, as well as a passionate hiker and backpacker.

After we arrived and parked the camper in their driveway, we got out of our truck and following the introductions, I meekly asked, "Do you have any pets?" I was experiencing my own post-traumatic stress from listening to the tales of the Iraqi cat just a few days before.

Nancy responded. "Yes, we have a new dog we recently rescued from the shelter. Her name is Zinger. I'm afraid that she doesn't like people. She'll try to nip at you."

Oh Lord, here we go again! And Tom had scheduled us for a three-day visit.

Zinger managed to live up to her reputation, furiously coming at us with every move we made, and while the two army buddies, Tom and Bud, went off to reacquaint themselves with each other and reminisce, Nancy and I were left to get to know each other, whether we wanted to or not.

Their home was a very large and beautiful Colorado ranch-style home, exquisitely designed and decorated with exciting colors and one-of-a kind artwork that Nancy had acquired over the years. She and I sat in the kitchen for a while, making small talk, but as the minutes passed, I quickly began to sense her irritation with having been stuck with me, or so I felt. And sure enough, it wasn't long before Nancy abruptly announced that she was going to go into her study to read.

Of course, I wasted no time in making a beeline for our camper before Zinger, the wonder-nipper, caught wind of my abandoned status. Truth be told, I was relieved when Nancy excused herself as it freed me to rest after days of traveling. Yet I also felt miffed at the same time, sensing that I had been dismissed. I suspected that my presence was more of an imposition than a fun, social event. I was starting to feel less than welcome. Pissed, really. Imagine that.

I had learned over the years that traveling with Tom usually meant stopping to visit anybody and everybody that ever passed through his

THE CAMPER'S GUIDE TO OUTRUNNING ...

life, but this merry outlook of his was starting to get old fast. And so there we were for the next three days. Bud took on the duty of host and of meal preparation while Tom and I tried to be exemplary guests clearing the table, loading and unloading the dishwasher—you know, halo stuff.

Given Bud's health status, Nancy became our tour guide and chauffer, showing us around the area and filling us in on historical and environmental details. She was really quite knowledgeable about these things.

I would like to point out that, while I am by nature a very reserved person until I have established a zone of comfort, I did put forth great effort from the backseat of Bud and Nancy's Subaru to comment enthusiastically on her tour guide information. I shared my touristic observations regarding, say, rock formations, and avidly asked highly intellectual questions regarding best restaurants or city population stats. But the woman never responded with any sort of comment whatsoever, as if everything that rolled off my tongue was of such blasé quality that it did not merit even the weakest of grunts. As I said before, it was really starting to get on my nerves.

So that night in our trailer, I shared my dislocated nose with Tom. "I don't know if she feels put upon by our visit or that I'm not up to her level of education and intelligence, or what, but it's starting to tick me off."

"You know," said Tom, "I have noticed that, too. I'm not sure what's going on."

This was a first for Tom. He is usually so jovial and easygoing that he simply cannot grasp the concept that there could be even a tad bit of grumpiness in the world.

"Well, perhaps we should cut our visit short," I suggested, with the greatness of indignation, not to mention drama. "The message I believe we are getting is that this isn't a good time for them to have visitors. So why don't we just put them out of their misery and relieve them of our imposition." By now, my nose was so high in the air that it was catching everything from mosquitos to fly balls.

"I don't know." Tom hesitated. He didn't have the knack of snootiness that I had cultivated over my lifetime. But not to worry; I had enough for the both of us.

PAT KANIS

I marched on. "We can tell them at dinner that we've made a change in our itinerary," I said. "We'll say that we've decided to spend tomorrow touring downtown Denver and then head on out of town from there. OK?"

"Yes," he said. "You're right. It's probably the best plan." God bless him.

To say that one of us chickened out on this "best plan" would be an understatement. It also would suffice to say that the same one of us who chickened out threw the other to the wolves. I'm not saying which one of us it was in order to prevent steam from reemerging from all orifices, but at dinner, when our hosts asked us what we would like to do the following day, Tom sat there in total paralysis staring at me, his lips apparently superglued together by his mashed potatoes. Thus, I was thrown into the spotlight by Chicken Little and forced to present Bud and Nancy with our change of plans.

"Well," I began, "Tom and I talked it over last night and have decided that we would very much like to see Denver. So we will be leaving tomorrow morning for Denver, and then we'll continue our journey east from there." I was not apologetic, but firm and steadfast, a real tower of authoritative strength.

The resulting objections from our hosts were hurled across the table like hot lava rocks from a sling shot, and as I ducked, I turned to Mr. Chicken Little for backup but received none. And so, after a conciliatory discussion, plans were made for a hike together the following day resulting with our departure from Golden on Monday, as originally planned.

The night was a chilly one in the ol' camper that night.

On the last evening of our stay, we sat around the table out on their patio talking about this and that—the daily bird kill from collisions with their large picture window, the wildfires that were plaguing the area, and how Zinger had managed to snatch nearly all the sausages from the kitchen counter and wolf them down. Then the conversation turned to their new patio and how very pretty everything was. Great care had been taken with regard to landscaping, potted flowers, rockery, and such.

"I designed this patio myself," Nancy said with pride, "and just now finished it. It took a lot of time and effort, but it's been something that I have always wanted. The rock used for the patio floor had to be special ordered and took months to arrive. It was also quite expensive. I had to choose between my hearing aids or finishing the patio. So I chose the patio...for now."

Tom and I glanced at each other.

Nancy continued. "I am legally deaf, as you've probably noticed. I get by all right with lip reading for now. Hearing aids are pretty expensive."

Tom faced Nancy and said weakly, "Why, no...I mean, we didn't realize..."

I don't think that I could have felt any lower than I did at that moment. I felt doubly so, knowing that Tom, who was never one to thinking poorly of anyone, had been dragged into this lowly practice by me.

Me, me, me...it's always about me.

I had broken all four of the agreements. I had not been impeccable with my word, having thought badly of Nancy and tempting Tom to agree with an unkind judgment.

I had selfishly taken Nancy's behavior personally, only to discover later that her actions had nothing to do with me at all.

I just took it on myself to make the assumption.

It wasn't my best.

Tom and I were quiet that night in our camper bed, but the next morning on our way out of town, he looked at me and softly said, "Well, she might have told us earlier." I smiled weakly as I had been still deep in self-flagellation. I am a great self-flagellator.

"And," he added, "I agree with you that the timing of our visit was probably just off for them."

And that was all that was said about that.

Lesson learned.

5

The Danger Zone

I was walking one morning along our neighborhood walking/biking trail, the kind that once was a train track in the glory days of railroads, when I was passed on my left by a bicycler. I mean a serious bicycler...the kind with a multimillion dollar titanium bicycle, wearing seriously revealing spandex shorts, a shirt advertising some past cycling event known only to serious bicyclers and pedaling four thousand revolutions per second, going further, faster, sleeker...whatever.

Now, any conscientious citizen, like me, knows that the "rule" on all former-railroad asphalt is that, just like on the road, everyone stays to the right and that if they need to, and when safe, may pass on the left.

Additionally, there are several signs along the route reminding those who don't understand—generally male bicyclers under the age of thirty—to "Give audible signal when passing."

I can't tell you how much these signs spark my imagination.

Give audible signal when passing. What type of "signal?" Whistle? Snap your fingers? Holler?

Furthermore, when passing what? The buck? Go? Gas?

Well, on this particular outing, and after the biker respectfully indicated that he was passing me "on your left," I spotted a young mother on the trail out ahead coming toward me. She was pushing a baby in a stroller, and along with them were three preschoolers on their wee little trikes. Oh, so cute!

I observed that the biker also eyed the mother and her miniature charges and cautiously slowed his pace, realizing that little sprouts tend to live in their own worlds and, accordingly, are very unpredictable.

And sure enough, once the tykes spied the bicycler coming toward them, all panic ensued. One tiny tot went right, one went left, one froze in place and however it all happened, they managed to all end up smack in the middle of the trail in one big heap of bicycles, helmets, elbows, knees, ankles and whatever else could have scraped the pavement. Tears followed with wails of, "Ow-ee," "Oh, my toe" and "She's on my arm,"—dramatic stuff like that. The mother, in calm charge, simply told them all to get up and out of the way of the oncoming biker. No sissy maker was she.

Recollection of this event brings to mind our trip down I-70 east toward, well the East Coast. We had left Golden, Colorado, one Monday morning and at some point just into Kansas, Tom asked me to find a place where he could pull his truck and trailer off the road, as there were two semis breathing down our necks. Being the ever-vigilant copilot, I looked for an obliging historical marker, view point or "dump your old car, sofa, appliances, and so forth here" site, when what to my wondering eyes should appear, but something climbing out of the nearby field and onto the road.

"Deer!" I yelled to Tom. Actually, it was a pair of antelope, which in all honesty, having been raised a city girl, I thought lived only somewhere in Africa. I had always wondered why they were included in the classic American folk song "Home on the Range."

Given our quandary of having two speeding semis baring down on us and two wildlife wanderers in front of us, for a split second, visions of the preschooler pile up came to mind but quickly changed to alarm of more mammoth proportions, similar to a free-fall skydive gone awry.

Fortunately, the antelope changed their itinerary and retreated into the field just in the nick of time, allowing the color to return to Tom's face, not to mention fingers, lips, eyeballs, and well, balls in general.

It wasn't long before we were able to find a safe place to pull off the road and allow the beat-the-clock bruisers to pass us.

Continuing down adventure road, we turned on the radio—I don't know why. You really can't hear anything when traveling in a pickup anyway—and heard that a tornado had touched down at the Denver airport earlier that morning. We marveled about how lucky we were,

Wow! We had just passed that area on our way out of Colorado that very morning!

Unfortunately, we would be retracting that high five soon enough. After all, does the weather not usually move west to east? Were we not also moving west to east?

Ambling along, we put a goodly amount of mileage away that day, noting how the landscape gently rolled out from hilly to flatter and admiring the mile after mile of wheat and barley, until landing at a campsite on a bluff overlooking the reservoir at Wilson Lake. The weekend revelers had retreated by then and peace was ours.

The following day of Tom and Pat's great adventures, we left I-70 and ventured south and then east in search of the Tall Prairie Grass National Monument—Tom's idea. He saw it on the map. I was sure that no one else had ever heard of it. It was a blue-sky morning that heated to one billion degrees in no time, and by the time we finally reached the monument a few hours later, I was wilting. I also noticed that some impressive thunderheads were starting to build.

Ever alert for climatic changes—after all, we were in Kansas—I said, "Tom, I don't like the looks of those thunderheads coming this way."

And Tom, ever the resolved optimist, simply responded in his usual manner of denial, the way he responds just before we get into really big trouble. "Nah, those are nothing. We're OK."

I looked at the sky again and pressed on. "Tom, you grew up in California. I grew up in Ohio. I think I know my clouds."

THE CAMPER'S GUIDE TO OUTRUNNING ...

The fact was that, like Joni Mitchell, I really didn't know clouds at all. But I was very sensitive to impending danger on the horizon. Yes siree.

While I went back into the trailer to find us some lunch, Tom went into the visitor center to use the men's room. Men his age always have to use the men's room. When he returned he was grinning ear to ear, eager to report to me some thrilling information.

"I talked to the girl at the counter in there. She says that she has worked here every summer for the past three years while on summer break. She told me that the storms never come down here. They always follow I-70 east."

"Oh for heaven's sake, Tom," I exclaimed. "Now you're getting weather facts from the college temp help? Is she the summer weather psychic? 'Storms always follow I-70 east.' That is the most preposterous thing I have ever heard. Weather goes where it is destined to go, generally based on atmospheric influences, not interstate traffic!"

Tom shrugged his shoulders, chowed down his ham and cheese, and then, eager to explore, said, "Let's get going. The path starts just over there past the visitor center." He was high with the anticipation of tall prairie grass viewing.

So we headed down the path. It was all very exciting, sort of like strolling through a neighbor's yard that hadn't been mowed in a very long time.

And it was hot. Really hot. A billion degrees hot.

And did you know that grasshoppers bite? One got caught up in my loosely flapping white blouse that I was wearing to shield my aging skin from the potential damaging effects of the sun's UV rays, after years of youthful, baby-oil drenched sunbathing. I felt a painful bite on the back of my shoulder and instinctively gave it a whack! Out dropped the grasshopper, but not before staining my not-so-freshly-ironed white blouse with its innards. I'm in hell.

We plodded along admiring the—well—nothing, there and back. And I don't have to tell you that by the time we had reached our truck-and-trailer fun pack, the "nothing-to-worry-about" thunderheads were definitely worry worthy.

"Tom," I said as we climbed into our pickup. "I read that there is a nice RV park back up on I-70 in Topeka. It says here in the Good Sam's Club book that it is highly rated and that it has a storm shelter. I think that we should head back up that way instead of the way that you've planned."

Tom, ever the adventure seeker, had scheduled us to dry camp at little hideaways along I-35, traveling east-northeast toward Kansas City. I, the traveling companion by marital default, following along with minimal enthusiasm for cross-country camping travel, had somewhat obliged him in his quest to outrun the grim reaper. But in this case, I was determined to play the safety card.

"Really?" he asked.

"Yes," I replied emphatically. "I would feel a lot better camping somewhere with a storm shelter, given that the skies are beginning to look ominous."

Tom sighed with disappointment. He's good at sighing with disappointment, but I pressed on.

"Just down the road due east is the entrance to the turnpike (toll road) that will take us directly up to Topeka." I pointed the route out on the map. Eventually—and reluctantly—he agreed to change course.

No sooner had we turned onto the toll road, rounding the very first bend, and there it was, a solid wall of black extending west to east as far as the eye could see, and coming right toward us. Our faces froze as we tried to comprehend what we were about to drive into. Neither of us spoke.

Additionally, at that very moment the NOAA weather alarm, purchased previously at my suggestion and now tucked safely in my purse, went off alerting us to our impending doom. The alarm warned us of a severe thunderstorm traveling NW to SE and impacting such-and-such counties through which, of course, we were currently passing and/or about to pass.

The alarm continued to advise us of the possibility of damaging winds up to eighty miles per hour and golf ball–size hail. We were instructed to seek shelter immediately in an interior room, and—you know—hair-raising warnings.

Well, guess what? There was no shelter around. In fact, the last sign we saw indicated that the next exit was forty miles away. No exits. No culverts. No houses. No playmates with cellar doors.

With the rain, wind, and hail coming down so strongly, not only was it impossible to hear inside our truck, but it was impossible to drive. We looked for an overpass under which to take shelter—I have since been told by several people that you should never seek shelter under an overpass—but they were all occupied by other struggling drivers. So we quickly pulled over onto the shoulder.

Tom started swearing about the possible damage to his truck and new camping trailer. I, however, remained cool and rational despite visions of Dorothy and Toto's hard landing into Oz. When the storm eased a bit, we, and the rest of the traffic, started up again only to be forced to pull over seconds later. This scenario repeated itself for quite some time.

In the meantime, the weather alert in my purse kept screeching. Now, however, something very noteworthy caught my attention. The announcer was saying that the storm was traveling from northwest to southeast at five miles per hour.

Hmm. My brain began to calculate with the exactitude and velocity of that of Albert Einstein.

"Tom," I said. "NOAA is saying that this storm is traveling at five miles per hour."

By this time, Tom was so unnerved that I was actually the calm in the storm for a change.

"As soon as the rain eases again, let's make a run for it," I said.

"What?"

"We can outrun this," I explained. "We are traveling from southwest to northeast at approximately fifty miles per hour and the storm is advancing from northwest to southeast at five miles per hour. We can outrun this!"

I always come through in a crisis, strong as a rock and dependable, saving humankind—or in this case—my man's travel trailer.

Tom scratched his smooth head and then watched as the rain ease up again. Once again, the traffic started moving slowly and so did we. We proceeded safely, but with determination, and in no time at all we had outrun the storm, rolling into the safe hands of Deer Creek RV Park of Topeka, Kansas, at quarter to six.

The first thing I asked the young woman at the desk upon check-in was, "Where is your storm shelter?"

"The restrooms," she replied.

Good enough.

Now I realize that the general population of Kansas would not consider this semidaily summer occurrence a hair-raising phenomenon, but we're from western Washington, land of heavy-metal skies and daily drizzle. What we had just experienced was nothing less than traumatic. OK, probably not traumatic, but greatly unsettling, for certain.

This past summer, we were talking to friends who had just returned from a car trip to Iowa for a family reunion. They showed us pictures they had taken with their smartphone of the storm they had encountered when passing through Kansas. It looked familiar.

Been there. Done that. Piece of cake.

As a matter of fact, on the previously described cross-country traveling excursion of ours, we ran into stormy weather in Colorado and all through Kansas, Missouri, Iowa, Illinois, Indiana, Ohio, and again on our return trip through Wisconsin, Minnesota, South Dakota, Wyoming, and Montana.

After a while, the whole thing started to get old and rather tedious. Somewhere outside of Ohio, I stashed our infamous NOAA weather alarm (never to be turned on again) securely in a drawer in our travel trailer.

6

Running Out of Wall

couple of years ago, on a return trip from visiting Tom's sister in Boise, Tom and I took a detour into Hell's Canyon. That's right, Hell's Canyon. It's actually a national recreation area that straddles the Snake River, which borders both Idaho and Oregon. Although at the time the weather was wicked hot, like Tom, I looked forward to seeing some of the awesome scenery so prevalent in that area. (I meant that Tom also looked forward to the scenery, not that Tom is wicked hot. Well, actually, he is, but that's not the subject here.)

Anyway, with map in hand and a bit of guidance from Tom's sister, we headed west in our pickup along a nicely paved road, through a small town and up the gently rolling hills. The mountain meadows through which we eventually meandered were carpeted with thousands of lavender-blue lupine, which we found amazing. The scenery and views were absolutely spectacular, with plenty of "oo-ing" and "ah-ing" on our part.

Progressing onward and upward, the nicely paved road eventually gave way to a gravel road, then a dirt road, and then a very narrow, gravely dirt road. Up and up, around and around. The higher we went, the shorter the curves and the narrower the road. Soon we found that the road had tapered to the point of accommodating just one vehicle one way. I also observed, as the case almost always is when driving obscure mountain roads, that the drop-off edge of the road was on the passenger side. That is to say, that the new view out my window was straight down into oblivion. A shear rock wall on the left, oblivion on the right.

"Did we miss the sign warning us about the limits of this road? I didn't see any sign. Did you see a sign, Tom? Was there a sign?"

I was getting a bit edgy. Needless to say, I was sweating like an athlete in a steam room and trying not to decline into a Gladys Kravitz mode of hysteria. Tom was starting to twitch a little, although he kept insisting that we were OK and that this was nothing. And it all went well, until we rounded the next tight curve and looked straight into the windshield of an approaching pickup truck. Remember, ascending wall on the left, descending cliff off the right.

Both Tom and the other driver brought their trucks to an abrupt stop, a very prudent reflex in my opinion, and surveyed the immediate situation. All communication between the two drivers was via eye signals. Not a word was spoken.

To begin, each driver rolled down his window and retracted his side mirror. Then, each driver pulled as far to the right as safely possible, which I might say, was lovelier for the other guy, given that Tom and I were edging toward death's free fall to the basement level.

Slowly, the trucks began their creep forward, inch by inch, drivers' attention glued to the slippery trail under them. No sound, just that of the slow revolution of rubber against pebble and the weak, but steady breaths of each passing driver.

Then it was over. The death-defying rite of passage had been successful. We had survived! Yes, indeed, we were alive! When we reached the bottom of the pass, I pried my right hand from the door's armrest allowing blood to return and began to breathe again. By the time my speech capabilities had resumed, my husband was learning about the true meaning of Hell's Canyon and debating with himself about the actual benefit of his survival status.

While we continued onward on our canyon exploratory experience, my mind began to wander, as it always tends to do, and I thought about walls: walls that lead straight up, while others lead straight down; walls that are put up, walls that are taken down, climbing up walls, climbing over walls, climbing down walls; looking over walls, leaning against walls...

— ～

I have two daughters who are over six years apart in age and different as night and day. As any parent will attest to, nothing gives you more insight into just what life is all about as watching children go through the growing process.

When my firstborn was learning to walk, I watched her crawl over to chairs, sofas, coffee tables, human legs, or whatever and pull herself up. Then she would practice balancing a bit before sitting straight down with a thump. Pretty soon, she was successfully—and proudly—balancing on her own. The first steps and tumbles followed, but in no time, she was on her way to mischief, exploring, and getting into anything and everything that caught her eye—you know, typical baby-toddler behavior.

My youngest daughter, however, chose a more tentative and cautious route. On her first attempt at converting from knees to feet, she crawled up to an available wall and hand-walked herself up to her feet. There she stood, face-to-face with the wall. Being the ever-so-sharp baby that she was—takes after her mother—she realized that getting back down was a scary prospect, and so would stand at the wall until her signal whine brought Mom to the rescue to sit her back down.

After a few days of this process, having thoroughly thought out a new plan, she began to hand-walk up the wall, steady her balance, and then carefully start sidestepping to the right. This was a very ingenious, albeit safe, way to execute the maneuver, and I sat marveling at the baby's thought process. I also noticed that, sooner or later, she would run out of wall, which meant that a possible catastrophe hung on the horizon. Because of the alert mother that I am, I got into a habit of timing my attention to her according to the length of the wall. As soon as my soon-to-be toddler arrived at the point of the crash site, I would dash over and remove her from said wall, placing her safely down on her bottom, only to have the process begin anew.

As you might have guessed, this whole routine got old really fast. It wasn't too long until I thought to myself, "You know, we'd all like to make it to home base without a scratch, but even I know that if you want to win the game badly enough, sooner or later you'll have to slide in, even if it hurts, gravel and all."

So the next time I eyed my little one closing in on the wall cliff—well—what can I say? I let her tumble. In my defense, your Honor, the point of impact was carpeted. As was expected, she did not much appreciate this change in outcome.

I picked her up, gave her some lovin', scanned her for injuries, and then put her back down. You know the rest. Crawl up, sidestep, fall down. Crawl up, sidestep, fall down. It really didn't take long before her rapidly developing brain signaled the end of this pattern. In other words, *Enough of this*. And in no time, she, too, took off on two feet toward toddler adventure.

— ⌣ —

Babies aren't the only ones who go through the process of learning how to walk.

I met Tom one year after he had lost his wife to cancer. She died unexpectedly following a surgery, leaving Tom to deal with his loss and life on his own. At first, he attached himself to me like a wet leaf, desperate not to be left alone. And as with my babies, I watched him take small steps...hesitant, unsure, reluctant, but knowing in his heart that he had no real choice. If he was going to go on, despite all doubts, he needed to put one foot in front of the other and fake it until he made it. It wasn't easy. It was never easy.

In the first couple years of our relationship, I frequently came to visit Tom at his home and, walking in the front door, I would find him sitting in his recliner in agony, consumed with acid reflux and gasping for air. At first, as with my daughter, I wanted to catch him. I wanted to help him through the hurt, to soothe him, to make it all better. What can I do? Do you need more antacids? Baking soda? I sat on the floor next to him for hours, until the attacks subsided.

But to be completely honest about the situation, I will share that soon it dawned on me that these attacks of Tom's always came around seasons or anniversaries of emotional attachment—Christmastime, his late wife's birthday, the anniversary of her death—which were painful, extremely painful.

After a while, I reluctantly confessed to myself that I could not rescue Tom. I could not live, experience, or alleviate his pain. I could not make it go away. This was personal only to him. This was his life, his loss, his grief. As we all know, try as we may, we all eventually run out of wall. We all fall.

Tom was standing up, but he would have to take the steps on his own, or he would never be able to learn how to walk again.

I had no choice but to stop making a big deal over Tom's acid attacks, and over time they did subside. Tom eventually hit his stride and found his peace.

I love this man like no other.

7

Looking for Mrs. Good Time

Tom knows that I love to swim—not indoors, but outdoors, in the warm sunshine. When I was a child, swimming in big, clear, warm lakes was the highlight of all our family camping excursions. So during Tom's and my cross-country travel-trailer travels—try saying that three times—he is always on the lookout for campsites that have a great place to swim. What can I say? My man likes to please me. Sadly, the feat of locating wondrous swimming opportunities has not always been that easy.

One of the more "fascinating" places we found was at a campsite in mid-Ohio, named Something-or-Other View Recreation. We arrived in the late afternoon, tired, hungry, and hot. It was a very pleasant camping spot—clean and not wall-to-wall crowded—although I'm not so sure about the "view." But what excited me most about this place was that, as we pulled in, I spotted what looked to be a beautiful swimming lake. At least I think it was a lake. More like a small pond, perhaps. But from a distance, it looked blue, clean, and crystal clear! I couldn't wait to strip—try not to envision this—put on my swimsuit and head on down the path for a refreshing dip.

Faster than you could yell, "Cannonball!" I was at water's edge. The beach was sandy, which I deduced must have been imported from, I don't know, a nearby agricultural sand machine or something, and the water was blue. I mean a bright, turquoise blue. I should have listened to my native Buckeye intuition on this one, because a turquoise-colored pond in mid-Ohio didn't make a lick of sense. But still, I dove in and cooled my weary bones.

It was not crowded. In fact, there was only one young woman and her ten-year-old daughter in the water splashing about. A small, friendly chat morphed into a twenty-minute ear bending until I finally extracted myself, politely referring to dinnertime.

When I came out of the lake-pond, I noticed that the water dripping from me onto the sand was turquoise. The water spots on my beach towel that I used to dry off with were also turquoise. I couldn't run to the shower fast enough to hose off all remnants of the tinted lake-pond, lest my recently, every-so-stylishly colored hair suddenly convert to old-lady blue.

Tom, who eons ago majored in animal science or something similar, suggested that the water's turquoise tint must have been some type of added antibacterial agent, since this was not a freshwater lake-pond. He had seen it used with cattle.

Thanks loads.

Moving right along, our second-most fascinating swimming experience during our cross-country trip occurred at a campground in Bremen, Indiana. This one also had a swimming pond, but it was not turquoise. It was a brown pond, and therefore, a bona fide pond. Honestly, it did not really beckon me for a cool dip, but there were many families with kids in the pond seeming to be having an extraordinarily great time. So Tom and I decided to check it out.

We walked around the circumference of the pond, glancing at the kids on their floats who were enjoying water-splashing competitions. At that same time, I noticed something ahead of me lying on the path along the shore. An up-close inspection proved that it was a dead frog.

"Ick, Tom! Look at this."

He came to inspect it, replying, "Hmm." We walked on.

Soon enough, we came upon another dead frog, then another, and still another. I did not find dead frogs particularly enticing for a re-freshing swimming experience. Still, with Tom's encouragement, as he was so eager for me to be excited about swimming, I removed my flip-flops and waded into the pond...up to the top of my ankles in muck.

Next!

Onward into Wisconsin, we hit the jackpot near Milton. Talking about a jumping place! A very pretty campground resort, which ap-peared to be very clean and packed with campers—it was Fourth of July weekend. We observed that, apparently, the park was so big that the aver-age family could not walk the one hundred paces to the swimming pool, or anywhere else for that matter, as everyone there employed the use of motorized golf carts of some sort to get around.

We were enthusiastically informed upon check-in that we had ar-rived just in time for adult swim hour—that is, no kids allowed. My heart started racing. So what if it was a pool. My experience so far with lake-ponds had left me drooling for a nice, clean, refreshing, chlorine-filled, bona fide swimming pool. What's more, after hour upon hour of driv-ing, my body cried out for exercise. Cool, buoyant, sun-filled exercise, muscle-celebrated front crawls, back crawls, side strokes—everything I had ever learned during PE in the pool at Goodyear Junior High school.

After what felt like an eternity of focusing on squeezing our travel trailer into its assigned two-by-four spot, Tom and I both donned our gay swimming apparel and raced toward the pool for the adult swim hour. Well, I guess I wouldn't exactly call it a swim. Adults, yes. Swim, no. With the exception of a two-square-foot spot in the middle, the pool was full to capacity of standing adults. I mean overflow full: standing, happy, chatting adults with one hand hanging onto the side of the pool and one holding some type of beverage. And to make it even more fes-tive, there was live karaoke. Oh, the gaiety of it all!

Given that there would be no laps today, we put our blanket and tow-els over on the grass and made our way into the revelry of the pool, Tom and I each finding a spot along a wall on which to cling. Kicking our legs back and forth in an effort to feign exercise, we listened to typical karaoke country songs such as "Crazy," "On the Road Again," and "For the Good Times."

Alas, before our fingertips even had a chance to reach a waterlogged wither, adult swim hour came to an end. While children began to line up around the circumference of the pool's edges in anticipation of the end of adult swim, Tom and I made our way to the lawn to dry off. Suddenly, all present - adult, children and karaoke singers - began to stand at attention

"I wonder what's going on," I said to Tom. I was mystified.

He shrugged.

Nevertheless, we joined the others and stood up. Tom pointed. The American flag positioned next to the pool was being lowered, and as it was, all present covered their hearts with their right hands. Again, Tom and I followed suit lest we appear as out-of-towners.

The man at the karaoke microphone started up with the National Anthem and all of the saturated swimmers joined him. ": Oh say can you see....?"

Tom and I looked at each other. Our eyes met in a silent "Where are we?"

Don't get me wrong. Tom and I are as loyal and patriotic as the next people, but the lowering of the flag in the middle of the afternoon, at the end of adult swim hour, accompanied by our national anthem, well it just took us a teensy bit by surprise. I guess you could say that it was an unexpected curiosity.

Later that evening, while I was resting semi-comatose inside the trailer, Tom flung open the door and hollered in, "Pat! You've got to come out and see this."

Reluctantly I left my oasis of pillows and magazines and ventured back outdoors. Up the dusty road in the dusk came a parade of golf carts and bicycles all decorated with lights, streamers, balloons, music, and kids all waving with excitement in the pride of their splendor. I watched in amazement—disbelief, really.

Tom was all smiles. "Isn't this something?" he asked excitedly. I believe that we were the only parade spectators, as it looked as if the entire camp population was involved in the joyful display.

"Yes," I replied, "very nice, and very, well...Midwest." A total sourpuss response if ever there was one, I admit.

Just between you and me, I have been wondering for quite some time now, the last couple of years in fact, why simple things just don't seem to thrill me anymore the way they used to. Why does my heart not jump right into celebrations and merrymaking? What does it take now to make me feel electrified, ecstatic, or high—without the assistance of pot or other mood-altering temptations, of course...yes, of course?

How have I become so difficult to impress? Is this some type of post-menopausal malaise, the incentive behind the stampede of older men toward the excitement of our more energetic younger sisters?

Still, I know plenty of women my age and older who work full time and hike, run marathons, volunteer for umpteen different organizations, go to yoga class followed by Zumba, followed by lap swimming, and on and on. My best friend, Kathryn, is two years older than I am and continues to be a world traveler—the more dangerous the destination, the better. She is also a daytime nanny, cooks gourmet dinners, and is as chipper and enthusiastic a person as I have ever known.

So what's with the blasé attitude? Is this what they call depression, or am I just basically a dull woman?

In past years, whenever at a party, holiday dance, or social gathering with people who appeared to be genuinely having a great time, there would often be one person—generally someone's husband—sitting at our table, who looked bored and would mumble about how phony everyone was behaving. But I never believed that to be true. I just felt that every now and then adults have to turn their worries off and their playfulness on. Otherwise, we'd all go crazy.

So why is my inner child choosing not to come out to play now? I feel more like the school playground woman than the kid on the swing.

Could it be possible that I have been living in the conservative Northwest so long, closed up in my house against the dark, the gray, and the rain so unnatural to me, that I've lost the incentive to have fun? Or has the definition of "fun" changed with age? Has the bar been raised, or has it been lowered? Does it now take more, or is it that it takes less?

Or perhaps it is that, as we mature and our eyes change—I'm not referring to cataracts here—so, too, does our vision. We develop a clearer perspective and see life from greater angles. We crave the extraordinary rather than the ordinary, not necessarily in order to outrun the grim reaper, but to outgrow him.

Hmm. This is a very profound thought indeed. I'll have to mull it over some more.

Meanwhile, what's the harm in enjoying a golf-cart parade now and then? It can't hurt. I can applaud and yell like the best of them.

8

The Purest Soul

*M*y husband talks to himself. No, I mean, he *really* talks to himself. No simple questioning—"Now where did I put that wrench?" No simple swearing—"Doggone slugs ate my whole crop of lettuce." Not even simple, quiet mumbling—"Mumble, mumble...could put some bleach in the wash once in a while." I mean out and out, loud and clear, direct conversations with himself.

When I first met him, whenever I heard him talking in the other room, I would just say something like, "What? Were you saying something to me?" and he would simply reply, "No, just talking to myself."

After a while though, after I *really* got to know him, I arrived at the realization that talking to himself was Tom's lifelong way of hacking his way through the tangled brambles of life. He just thinks aloud—really loud—a lot. There are occasions, though, when he is actually asking me a question and not talking to himself. And when I ignore what I assume is his self-talk, he, in return, is wondering if I'm beginning to lose my hearing.

You've all heard the joke, right, about the man who confides in his doctor that he believes that his wife might be going deaf? So the doctor gives him a good way of testing this possibility.

"When you're at home with your wife, stand in the next room," the doctor advises. "Ask your wife a question. If she doesn't respond, move down the hallway closer toward her and ask her again. If she still doesn't respond, move even closer. This should give you some idea of the extent of possible hearing loss."

So the man did exactly what his doctor instructed him to do. When the man's wife was in the kitchen cooking dinner one evening, the man called to her from the bedroom. "Hey, honey, what's for dinner?" No response.

So he walked a few paces down the hallway toward his wife and stopped. "Honey, what's for dinner?" Again, nothing.

Finally, he approached the kitchen entry. "What's for dinner, honey?" To which his wife responded, "For the third time, Henry, we're having chicken."

One day I was driving home from work and came into our neighborhood to find Tom walking up the street toward home, gums just a flapping. I could hear him through my closed car windows.

"You know, Tom," I said to him once he came into the house, "the neighbors are going to consider you the neighborhood loon if you keep that up. You just can't go walking around talking loudly to yourself like that, as if there were someone next to you."

Then I paused and gave it a moment of profound reflection. "Is there someone next to you, Tom?" I asked. "Do you, you know, see dead people?"

He rolled his eyes. "I just think more clearly when I talk things out with myself," he explained matter-of-factly, as if it were the most natural thing in the world, something that all people do, or at least should do. No big deal.

Tom discusses everything with himself: bills and finances, insurance decisions, his children's difficulties, my children's difficulties—even if all of said children are grown adults who are highly capable of attending to their own difficulties—my health, and that of every family member, to go skiing today or not, chocolate chip or oatmeal, pale ale or red wine...and on and on.

One evening, I heard him in the shower having an out-and-out, back-and-forth conversation about who knows what, and I poked my head in the bathroom door for the sole purpose of needling him.

"Do you have your imaginary playmate in the shower with you again?" I asked, feeling a bit ornery.

And without skipping a beat, he replied, "Yeah. Want to join us for a threesome?"

Bless his innocent, pea-pickin' heart. He must have overheard that term when I was watching an episode of *Sex and the City*.

— ~

Tom likes to talk in general. Whereas I am more of an introvert, Tom sees people as a wonderful gift from God, specifically put on this earth to converse with him. When we walk in to a social gathering, I can actually see his prefrontal cortex light up like a neon sign. Eeny, meeny, miny, moe...! He is very friendly.

What's your name again?
Oh, where are you from?
What do you do?
What does your wife do?
Are you originally from around here?
How many children do you have?
Where do they go to school?
Are your parents still living?
Are they originally from around here?
Do you ski?

What's more, Tom likes everyone. It doesn't matter about whom he is speaking, he always concludes with, "He is the nicest guy," or "She is the nicest person," or "They are the nicest people." He simply sees goodness in everyone.

Tom considers every single person that has ever crossed his path as his good friend—childhood friends, college friends, army buddies, summer ranching friends, colleagues from his job at the bank, colleagues from his work in the insurance industry, hiking buddies, and so forth. Of course, the best friend of all is the one person currently on the ski lift with him, trapped for a minimum of twenty minutes and all to himself. *So many questions; so little time.*

And need I ask you to guess who spends hours upon hours sending Christmas cards every holiday season to each and every one of these very best friends? You can bet your sweet fruitcake it's not me. I happen to have seven siblings, five good friends and a few aunts and uncles to whom I gladly contribute ten minutes each holiday season.

Needless to say, all of these good friends of Tom's all seem to live along the camp-across-America route, so we couldn't just blow through Oregon, Utah, Colorado, California, Iowa, Wisconsin, Montana, Idaho, and so forth, without "stopping to say hello" (translation: staying with them for a few days to sit for hours and hours, drink beer, and reminisce about the good old days), now can we? At least now that we have the camping trailer, it's not about the free lodging.

——— ——

Just for the record, I would like to say that every now and then, I can talk Tom into seeing the financial benefits of flying to certain destinations, and one of my favorite destinations is Siesta Keys, Florida. All white sand and warm, turquoise ocean, it is heaven on earth...in May.

I have to admit, though, that I don't particularly like to fly, but once my doctor prescribed Xanax-for-anxiety travel, since I don't drink, flying has become tolerable. And for some particularly odd reason that doesn't make a lick of sense, I actually feel more comfortable in the little commuter planes—I call them bumble bees—than in the huge jumbo jets, despite the safety and crash statistics. Go figure. But I digress.

I drag you into all of this to further explain to you my husband's genuinely pristine heart. On a return flight from Siesta Keys to Seattle through Houston, we ended up on a flight—airline carrier shall remain nameless for reasons forthcoming—that was, shall we say, at the least, trying.

Given that the industry continues to cut services—*Me help you put your bag up in the overhead? No way! I don't care how old or handicapped, you should have paid the thirty dollars to check it. I have my own back to think of.* And leg room—please keep your seats in an upright position at all times as, well, there is no downright position because there is no longer the least amount of room between passengers...greater profits for us...less circulation for your legs, butt, back, arms, and neck.

The whole boarding process proceeded very, very slowly with the flight attendants yelling and scolding and urging people to hurry up as we had a schedule to keep. They were bossing us all to step out of the aisle and into our seating area to let other passengers pass, knowing very well that to comply would pretty much eliminate any chance for the step-aside passenger to find a place to stow an overhead bag.

To say the procedure was tense is an understatement. But wait! It gets even more interesting. There appeared to be two very well-dressed passengers from South America who refused to sit in their assigned seats, as they preferred more leg room. So they just helped themselves to the front seats. One of the already hysterical flight attendants explained to the two passengers that they could not just pick out which seat they wanted. They had to sit in the seats they had been assigned to on their tickets.

This was not going to be an easy fix, as the two South Americans, apparent nobility traveling in coach, refused to budge. With two flight attendants now on the case, the rogue duo were informed that they needed to kindly follow one of the attendants out of the plane and that an alternative flight would be found for them. After ten stubborn minutes, the reluctant duo acquiescently accepted their assigned seats and sat down.

But wait! There's more. The doors to the plane started to close when the now totally unhinged flight attendant was tapped on the shoulder by a young man standing in the aisle. She turned to him and asked him to please take his seat.

"There is someone in my seat," he replied, presenting her with his ticket.

The flight attendant looked at the ticket and then looked back at the young man. "How did you get in here? You are on the wrong flight."

Security was called, much yelling and heated debating ensued pertaining to who was responsible for this breach, and eventually the young man was escorted off the plane to the appropriate flight.

After all of that and after everyone appeared—finally—to be seated, not to mention unnerved, the by-then-wreck-of-a flight attendant turned to the people in the cabin and asked, "Anybody else? May we depart now?"

Like 1950s parochial students faced with a red-faced nun, there was nary a peep, and we departed Houston bound for Seattle.

But wait...there's more.

Now you remember the part I told you about being crammed in like sardines, right? The part that I forgot to tell you was that, for some reason, Tom and I had tickets that required seat assignment upon check-in. What can I say? They were a "deal." As it turned out, my seat was up against a window, under the storage bin and next to and behind a group of sumo-sized men, while Tom was assigned several rows back on the other side of the plane in the emergency exit aisle seat, which was great for him as he has very long legs.

About a half hour into the flight, the sumo-sized man in front of me—also crammed up against a window and under a storage bin—started to fidget in his seat. After a few more minutes, he began to mutter to himself, "I can't do this. I can't do this."

Pretty soon, the muttering increased in volume and he screamed for the two sumo passengers next to him to please let him out. Once out in the aisle, he found *the* flight attendant—now a walking zombie—and told her that he was having a panic attack and needed a different seat.

"There are no other seats, sir. You will have to sit in the seat assigned to you. Please sit down."

"I can't! I can't. I can't breathe! I can't breathe! I can't sit there!

I guess we could all agree that this definitely was a convincing display of a panic attack.

By this point, there was only one solution. I unlocked my seat belt, twisted myself into a reverse position on my knees, and found Tom's face several rows back.

"Tom," I yelled. I might as well have yelled, "Listen up, everyone," because I, the introvert, had just yelled across and gotten the attention of the entire airplane. "The gentleman in front of me is having a panic attack," I continued. "He needs room. Will you change seats with him?"

You should have heard the reaction of this now weary traveling crowd. It was one, long, collective moan. However, I knew my husband. I knew there was no question of if he would give up his seat. I knew that he would arise to the occasion without hesitation, which is exactly what he did. He's simply that kind of guy.

"OK," he responded. Just like that.

He was up and out of his seat in a second, taking only a moment to grab his *National Geographic*. After much hugging and words of gratitude from the panic-stricken passenger, a Desert Storm veteran with PTSD, as well as from the equally panic-stricken flight attendant (no doubt currently residing at Shady Meadows Rest Home for some much-needed R & R), Tom took his new seat in front of me. Jammed up against the window under the storage compartment, he was offered complimentary beverages and happily spent the rest of the flight bending the ear of the sumo next to him, who in turn bent Tom's.

Don't you just love him? Don't you wish you could be his imaginary playmate?

9

My Cooking Is Like My Hair

O ne of the most important benefits of travel-trailer over tent
camping, other than the obvious private restroom facility, is the
joy of cooking. Well, I wouldn't call it joy, exactly, but let's examine the pros and cons, shall we?

Tent camping: slow-to-heat up propane cook stove with single
burner, a cooler with melting ice and limited meal options (hotdogs,
chili, lunchmeat and lukewarm milk), neighboring children running
through your dining area, and the long process of heating up water to
wash and rinse dishes. Add to that the self-imposed culinary limita-
tions of gluten-free, dairy-free, legume-free, low-sodium, low-sugar,
and low-saturated-fat dietary restrictions in a valiant attempt to stretch
life expectancy as far as it will stretch, like an old, brittle rubber band,
knowing very well that, eventually, it's going to snap, taking us with it.
But what the heck...got to give it our best shot, right?

Camping trailer: kitchenette with four-burner stove, refrigerator,
microwave, double sink, on-demand hot water, complete privacy, and
all the food you can stuff in your refrigerator and cupboards, including

chicken, steaks, rice, potatoes, and broccoli—you know, all that healthy stuff.

"Pancakes for breakfast, dear, or perhaps, eggs and hash browns?" The sky's the limit...more or less.

The fact that the cost of a tent is a fraction of that of a small trailer is not the issue here. We're talking sanity. We're talking the difference between, "Honey, do you want red wine or beer with your beef stroganoff?" versus "Your choice is canned Spaghetti-Os or Spam. Take it or leave it!"

All right, so that was just the cons of one and the pros of the other, I know. Nevertheless, to be fair, cooking on the road is never what you might call delightful, especially if the road has been long and hot.

We pulled our weary selves into a KOA in Salem, South Dakota, en route to the Badlands, and checked in at the main office. The staff was very accommodating and friendly and, after we'd completed our check-in, wished us a nice stay and handed us a complimentary fly swatter.

"Hey," I said to Tom, "we can use one of these." We didn't have one in our stash of camping paraphernalia and, what the heck! Free is free.

We had no idea what we were in for.

Tired and hungry, we went through the usual procedure of pulling into our assigned spot, leveling the trailer, hooking up utilities, and carefully opening the cupboards and refrigerator to steady anything that might have, because of shifting, become potentially lethal during transit.

As it was hot, I mean stinking hot, we opened all the windows, the door and vents, and turned on a fan to get some air circulation. Wearily, I started preparing for dinner, when the first of the flies appeared. As on past occasions of insect intrusion, I checked to make sure that the screen door was closed all the way, which it was. Then, I checked the windows to make sure that one of the screens there hadn't been inadvertently pulled open, but all were secure.

By that time there were about a half dozen flies buzzing around my head.

I called to Tom, who was still outside fiddling with something-or-other. "Tom, I'm going to shut the doors and windows and turn on the air conditioning. The flies are coming in."

"Really?"

Remember that it was about a billion degrees out, and although my first reaction was to respond with a grumpy, "No, after a second look I believe that they are flying tarantulas," I chose to simply shut the door, close up the windows and vents, and turn on the air conditioning.

But, and I swear to you that I don't know how, the flies kept coming in. I grabbed my free KOA fly swatter and put it to use, but these buggers were fast—really fast. By the time Tom came in, I had turned into a raving, fly-swatting lunatic. They were everywhere, coming in by the hundreds.

"Must be a feedlot close by," he commented nonchalantly. "What's for dinner?"

My glare must have made sit him down at the table to take up his map analysis. Meanwhile, I did what I could to start dinner, chopping vegetables, swatting at flies, boiling water for spaghetti, swatting at flies, stirring sauce, and swatting at flies. You get the picture. It seemed to be a futile task, as with every swat the fly population appeared to triple. They must have been crawling in through any and every crack in the siding.

Just about the time dinner was ready, I noticed several handfuls of flies—not my hands, but a figure of measurement—clinging to the mirror on the bathroom door as well as on the mirror on the wall behind the dining bench. Since an obvious out-and-out insect war had been declared without provocation or permission, I proceeded to attack the mirrors with the vengeance of a Black Friday shopper.

Tom looked up from his map to see his normally sweet wife now diabolically cackling with each sweet splat. Soon I started to taunt the little winged manure feeders, egging them on, enticing them to escape to freedom and never-never-land via the mirrors.

To say that I had single-handedly rid our camping trailer of the entire infestation would be a falsehood, but at least we were able to eat our dinner with synchronicity, one fork, and one swat, at a time. The fly invasion did not let up entirely until we pulled up camp the next morning and headed to our next destination, the Badlands, otherwise known as the Inferno. One hundred and three degrees. No shade.

Have you ever wondered who is responsible for that "freedom of the open road" myth?

Still, along our merry way down I-90 I found myself chuckling about the thesaurus of swear words that had come out of me while attempting to cook the previous night's repast, and it reminded me of something I had once told Tom.

If you have ever watched the movie *Like Water for Chocolate*, based on the novel by Laura Esquivel, then you can—perhaps—appreciate why I cringe every time my husband turns his energies toward baking a pie.

Tom loves pies, but keeps his consumption to pumpkin pie at Thanksgiving and lemon meringue pie once or twice during the summer. Plus, he limits the fix for his sweet tooth to homemade only, no imitation, artificially flavored, only God-knows-what's-in-it, doesn't taste like Mom's, store-bought pies for him. No siree, Bob.

After his late wife passed, Tom took up the cause of homemade or bust, and by the time I had met him, he had his preferred recipe in line. It was a combination of Grandma's, Mom's, and wife's, with just the right amount of sugar, spices and topping to his personal liking. But the crust was a different story. The crust was a beast of a different color.

Tom cannot make a decent crust to save his soul and therefore enlists my assistance in that area every time he makes a pie. Now, heaven knows, I'm no world-renown pastry chef—or any type of chef for that matter. My family will attest to that. In fact, my personal motto has always been, "My cooking is like my hair. I never know how it's going to turn out." And that's a fact. But I do admit that by some twist of fate, and if not pushed or hurried, I can make a pretty decent, flaky piecrust. Not a delight to look at, but pretty tasty.

So Tom and I have set up our pie routine, with me on crust and him on filling. To say that we have the practice down to an art would be a falsehood, however. On any given pie-making day, there always seems to be a lot of agitation in the kitchen during our attempt to recreate childhood culinary memories, and while I always remain the calmest and self-assured of crust creators, one of us always finds his or her way into a pan full of profanities, certain that failure is on the horizon.

"Tom," I once asked him, "have you ever seen the movie *Like Water for Chocolate?*"

"No," came his strained response. "You know I don't watch much TV."

And that is a fact. Whereas he watches a bit of the daily news, Tom mostly only watches the weather forecast...weather for breakfast, weather for lunch, and weather for dinner. And just to be absolutely, positively sure, he also looks up the daily forecast once or twice during the day on the Internet. It has gotten to the point that his family calls him if they want to know what the day's weather will be.

"Well," I continued, while working tranquilly and gently on my nothing-short-of miraculous flaky piecrust, "briefly, it's about a young Mexican girl who has been given the task of cooking all of the family meals and special-occasion feasts. And in this movie, it comes to light that the emotions of the cook, in this case the young girl, are transmitted through the food she cooks to all those who eat it. If she is sad, everyone at the meal is sad. If she feels sick, they all feel sick."

I couldn't tell if he was totally focused on his pie filling or simply tuning me out. It must have been the filling.

"So," I continued, "if I were you, I would take care to limit some of those "f" and "sh" words you're using on that pie filling, lest we have a dining table of swearing family members for Thanksgiving, especially swearing children under the age of ten."

On every such occasion, I also make a point of warning the family that this might happen, just so they are not taken by surprise.

10

ℋighs and ℒows

ℐf there's one thing that I've learned through my years of camping, it's that there are basically two types of campers: the nature enthusiast and the vacationer. You can tell the minute they disembark from their SUVs, minivans, or trucks what their camping type is.

The nature enthusiast arrives with a backpack, hiking boots, thick socks, convertible pants, wide-brimmed hat, sunglasses, water bottle, all-natural but useless bug spray, sunscreen, and energy bars.

The vacationer arrives with, first and foremost, a cooler of beer along with lawn chairs, awning, table cloth, clothesline, Frisbee, stereo, dog, some type of musical instrument, and a thousand relatives.

Because of its rainforest and plentitude of mountain peaks, Washington State gets ample amounts of both types in any given summer, July 15–August 15. The scenery is amazing, and if you are lucky enough to get into the mountains at the exact time of the annual wildflower bloom, you are in for an absolutely awesome experience, similar to that of Dorothy's poppy fields only infinitely more colorful and without the opiate effect.

On a recent camping trip to Hurricane Ridge on the Olympic Peninsula, we camped next to, or should I say right on top of a young family from New York. They seemed to be very excited about their trip to the Northwest and expressed their wonder over the beautiful scenery.

Tom asked them if they had visited Mount Rainier yet, the pride of Washington State at 14,409 feet, and both the husband and wife nodded, a bit hesitantly though. It seems that I am not the only one from back East that has a fear of heights. They admitted that they had traveled only so far up the road through Mount Rainier National Park, when at some point they pulled over to see how much farther up they had to go.

Getting out of their SUV, they cocked their heads back and looked way up to see only dots the size of pin holes. Those were cars. They turned their SUV back around, deciding that they had gone high enough, thank you very much.

My brother, Scott, and his family came out a few years back on their first trip west. We had decided to take them to a place called Noble Knob, which offers you-can-almost-touch-it views of Mount Rainier and accompanying beautiful meadows without the strenuous hike. After all, these were folks from Ohio. The trip to Noble Knob is a seven-mile climb of nearly five thousand feet up a bumpy, narrow, and winding gravel road "not suitable for trailers or RVs." That should sound familiar to you right there.

After we had all piled into Scott's rental car, we were only three or four minutes into our ascent when perspiration began to bead on my brother's forehead, and within a few seconds, he had put on the brakes, put the gear into park, got out, and said to Tom, "You drive." See what I mean?

The Washington Pacific coast is also greatly spectacular and worth a visit. It's not spectacular in a Cancun kind of way, but more like a Moby Dick kind of way. It is very rugged, windy, foggy, and often stormy. In fact, many travelers drive to the extreme northwest coastal point of the Olympic Peninsula just to experience this awesome gray energy. And that is just where Tom and I traveled to camp for a few days.

We found a rather secluded campground on the Native American reservation at Neah Bay, and at that time, other than the cabin dwellers (and I don't mean rustic cabins, either), we were pretty much the only campers there.

Naive woman that I am, I had planned on a very peaceful, relaxing few days sitting on the beach, reading a good novel and working on my own epic bestseller. Alas, that was not the case. You take bone-chilling winds, whirling sand, and sprays of sea salt, and what you end up with is pickled butt.

Read a book? It took only a few minutes of maritime relaxation in my squat-size beach chair before my eyelids were cemented shut. Even with my Ohio State Buckeye hoodie, over my hiking jacket, over my fleece ski underwear (do not be impressed by the "ski" thing for I spent seven years on the beginner run before bagging that thrill-seeking death wish) were no match for the seafaring elements.

After only ten minutes, I picked up all of my "I am *so* ready to relax on the beach" supplies and hauled my behind back to the trailer, where I shoveled, shook, and shimmied off all the sand and looked for something else to do besides get into the M&M's...again. There was no phone service. There was no Internet. There wasn't even an outdoor puppet show or sing-along. Furthermore, Tom had gone off down the road to explore, so there wasn't even a husband to talk to, which sometimes is a blessing, but not in this case.

I elected to grab my book and spent the rest of the evening relaxing inside. At about the time I started to feel a bit antsy, actually, out-and-out stir-crazy, Tom came in the door excited about some petroglyphs that he had discovered. Although information about petroglyphs had been mentioned in one of his hiking books, the info was vague. So for him it was a great discovery, possibly meriting him some type of noble award. As a result, he and I made plans to drive farther down the coast the following day for additional exploration.

As was the case with most nature hikes, we spent a whole lot of time marching up and down and through the mud, amid the brush, into the woods and over the hills, and round the bend. Until we arrived at the point at which—in order to get to the beach—we had to use a well-established rope to help lower us down the deep, slippery terrain. I understand that this is no big deal for those who choose hiking as a lifestyle, but for me it was rather unnerving, especially when I thought about the impending return ascent. Always thinking ahead, you know. Or should I say, worrying ahead?

As the old adage goes, experience is the best teacher. Years before, as a new arrival from the Midwest, I learned the hard way that, if one has plans to hike along the beaches of Puget Sound or the Pacific Coast, one must first consult the tide schedule. Apparently, the water advances and retreats there on some type of schedule, and if one does not plan accordingly, one might be in for a lengthy hike back through waist-deep saltwater or an impromptu shimmy up a very steep embankment. With that in mind, I had remembered to bring along a tide schedule on that day's walk.

Our execution of the descent to the beach went off without a hitch, and once on firm ground, Tom was attracted to some seastacks (large rock formations) he'd spotted a bit down yonder. So we began our sandy walk in the direction of said yonder.

Wet sand is not always the blissful experience portrayed in romantic movies, you know. Sometimes it's hard as a rock and hard on the back. Other times, it is soft and deep, tough to walk in, and hard on the back.

We marched for some time toward our destination, most of the time with our hiking boots on, picking our way carefully around seaweed, logs, and rocks, and other times barefoot, feeling the coolness of the sand and testing the frigidity of the ocean water. We looked for sea life such as orcas, dolphins, and seals, but seagulls were pretty much our prize for that day.

After about an hour, we arrived at the large ocean rock formation, which frankly had looked to be much closer than it turned out to be, and set about investigating in, around, and through every nook and cranny. It was pretty much your basic seastack. Tom is a much better explorer than I, and thus I was finished with my oceanic analysis within ten minutes of arriving and ready to start back. I also had my internal alarm tuned into the tide schedule in my back pocket.

Forty-five minutes later, including fifteen minutes for a PB&J sandwich, half an apple, one mandatory banana—per Tom, a daily must that keeps his muscles in tiptop shape—and some water, we commenced our return journey. You know from your own travels that, even if just to the mall, it feels like getting back takes ten times longer than getting there, an eternity, actually.

Walking and walking, shoes off, shoes on, jackets off, and jackets on.

Just as I was beginning to get nervous about the possibility that we might have passed the ascension rope and that we were consequently doomed for high tide annihilation, we reached the point of our previous beach entry and said rope.

I looked up. Honestly, the sheerness of the cliff did not appear to be as daunting as it had seemed to me when coming down hours earlier. So with Tom hauling the backpacks, we battened down our shoestrings and started up. Tom went first, as he is in better shape than I was. In addition, he's a male and consequently has some inborn gene that dictates his taking the lead.

"Just warn me if you lose your grip and slip so that I can move out of the way," I cautioned him.

"If I lose my grip and slip," he replied. "I'm counting on you to stop my free fall. You're my back-up plan."

Ha, fat chance of that! I am a five-foot nothing weakling, so images of my impeding anyone from doing anything are comical.

I was always the kid in the neighborhood first tagged during a game of "Black Sheep," got a C+ in PE for fitness (not even one chin up executed, although attempted), and had to enlist my younger sister to defend me from whatever bully marked me for terror, which really didn't take much. Admittedly, every now and then I liked to try my hand at being athletic or tough, but regretfully, that decision always ended up being a very painful move.

At first, the rope ascent up the hill was quite doable, but soon the task became more strenuous, and at one point, I was crawling on my belly, grunting, groaning, and cursing myself for not taking that beginning weights for women course offered at work.

Maybe when we get home I'll find one of those CrossFit gyms that I've been hearing about. I'll work my way up to bulky biceps, firm abs, and a tight ass. I'll go on to participate in a Tough Mudder and be the envy of every senior at the center.

Not.

Using my elbows and toes and slipping back only once or twice, ultimately I was able to finish this vertical trek. I got back on my feet, retrieved my pack from Tom, and resumed the return trip to camp, up and down and through the mud, amid the brush, into the woods and over the hills, and round the bend. Once back to our trailer, I was able to immediately locate the mother of all petroglyphs...M&M's, the reward for finishing my own Tough Mudder.

A few days later, Tom and I broke camp and headed south down the coast to Ocean Shores, a very popular area for tourists and vacationing families. Whereas inland, it was sunny and warm, beachside it was foggy, windy, and chilly. Once again, I tried the "relax on the beach and read" option, but some activities were just not meant to be.

We went for walks up and down the beach and once drove into town to look around. That's when I remembered the kite.

Being the ever-so-remarkable woman that I am, I remembered to pack our kite. Well, actually it was Tom's kite. Eleven years earlier, when Tom was courting me and I him, I had given him a basket of goodies for Easter, which included a kite. Well, it seemed like a fun idea at the time, but in the end, the kite was retired, with good intentions, to the trunk of the car, and that's where it remained until that day. I had remembered it at the last minute when packing the camper and so had retrieved it.

What better time to put it to use? It was not a sunny beach, but it was a nice windy beach.

Tom was sitting outside at the picnic table analyzing maps again, when I sprang my brilliant surprise.

"Look what I brought!" You would have thought that I was presenting a ten-tiered layer cake. Such was my giddy pride.

"What is it?" he asked.

"Well, it's your kite," I responded. "Don't you remember? It's the one that's been in the trunk of your car for nearly eleven years."

"Oh yeah." He put down his map. Now I had his attention.

I continued. "I thought you might like to take it to the beach today and give it a try. You do know how to fly a kite, don't you?"

His chest puffed. "Well, of course I do. I used to fly them all the time when I was a kid."

I nodded but did not remind him that he was way past being a kid.

So we left camp and made our way down to the beach where Tom embarked on figuring out how to assemble his kite. It took some doing, but in no time at all, he had a functional flying apparatus.

"What is it supposed to be?" I asked. You know, usually kites have some type of awe-inspiring emblem, like a super hero, or perhaps a sky-rocket. But I couldn't figure this one out.

He took a good look as it hung in his hand ready for launching. "I think it's a fish."

"A fish?" I drew better fish than that way back in kindergarten. This must have been a Picasso rendition of a fish.

This brings to mind my high school mascot, a dragon named "Chang"—which understandably might be considered inappropriate in today's society. I don't know. In my senior year, the senior adviser talked the graduating class into using our funds to commission a sculpture of the dragon from a local artist.

We all thought that was a pretty cool idea, until we finally saw the finished piece. We were young and not prepared for what appeared to be a giant-size lizard splattered on the outside wall of our school next to the front entry, head abnormally twisted flush to the side and arms and legs splayed out like the thing had been shot from a cannon with an unexpected direct hit to the building.

Poor Chang. We eventually got used to the sculpture once we matured. After all, it was art.

I watched Tom as he prepared the kite's inaugural flight. I hoped that he wasn't planning to run up and down the beach in an effort to accomplish this launch. Visions of tripping over some rock and hitting his head, or a collision with an oblivious small child flashed before my eyes. But I soon realized that I had nothing to dread, as after two head dives into the sand, the kite was successfully airborne.

You should have seen his face. Such was the pride of Tom's success. He spent almost an hour walking up and down the beach with his kite in tow, looking up occasionally in satisfaction, as if he had just single-handedly launched a space rocket with a satellite destined for Mars.

I can tell you one thing for certain: Washington's beaches are not always the sunniest of beaches, but they are beautiful and seemingly endless. And what they may lack in sunshine, they make up for in wind. Lots of wind. Enough to get a kite up and keep it up for as long as a man wants.

And as you know, for an older man, getting it up and keeping it up are extremely important.

11

There Is a Season

My friend, Molly, first introduced me to hiking years ago. Even today she likes to give me a hard time about our first outing together, reminding me and everyone present, how I showed up in new white tennis shoes, no backpack, no lunch, and no water bottle. I guess you can say that I was new to the sport.

I don't really understand why Molly was my friend. We used to be coworkers at a local public school. She taught sixth grade and I was, well, the detention lady. Stop laughing now! It's not like it was the career of my dreams, but it was important for me to be on the same daily schedule as my daughters. I admit, however, that it was extremely traumatic the first time I saw graffiti scrawled on a school wall indicating that "Mrs. _ _ _ _ is a b_ _ _ _. Well, perhaps it might have been true at the time.

When I say that I don't know why Molly was my friend, I mean that I don't why she became my friend. Molly was highly intelligent and had her master's degree. Not only that, she was very, very knowledgeable about so many things—not just reading, writing, and arithmetic, but all of those things that, if you wanted to find out about them, you'd have to research them. She was virtually an entire set of Encyclopedia Britannica in black pumps.

Molly was single but, for all practical purposes, had thirty plus kids... every year. She was very effective, genuinely appreciated by both staff and students, and somehow during the course of several years, she and I just fell into an enthusiastic friendship. The truth is that I think Molly sensed that I was very lonely, and therefore took me under her friendship wing to try to fill some of that emptiness.

Having grown up on the West Coast, Molly was an outdoor enthusiast. So not only did we take occasional (beginner) hikes together but also sometimes did the Audubon thing while taking walks down a trail with our binoculars (got me some new binoculars) or went on bike rides, and all of that other cool outdoor stuff.

By the way, did you know that a black bird with red on its wings is called a red-winged blackbird? I know! That's the kind of fascinating stuff that I learned while exploring nature together with Molly. She just knew everything about everything.

At the end of every school year, Molly would pack up and head out to visit family who were scattered among the western states. One early summer Saturday morning, I received a telephone call from her telling me that she had just finished loading up her car and was about to depart for her summer trip when she'd received a call from her brother telling her that her mother had taken ill and was on the way to the hospital.

"They don't yet know exactly what the matter is," she explained to me when she called, but I was wondering if you would be willing to lend me your cell phone so that I can keep in touch with the family during my drive."

This was at a time when cell phones weren't yet a global necessity. In fact, I hardly ever used my phone. It had limited minutes, thirty per month I think, and I only kept it for emergencies, really.

"Or course," I told her. "I hope that your mom's all right."

"I can mail your phone back to you as soon as I get there," she explained. "I really do appreciate this."

Understandably, she sounded agitated. "I am just about to leave now. I should be at your house in about twenty minutes."

After we hung up, I sat for a minute at my kitchen table feeling bad for Molly, when all of a sudden I heard a voice in my head saying, "Go with her."

I thought about how worried she must be. I wondered what the matter was with her mother and the urgency of the situation. The voice in my head wouldn't go away.

She probably wouldn't want my company along for the drive anyway, I rationalized. After all, she tends to be a very private person. Besides that, how would I get back?

Still the voice nagged at me: "Go with her."

It would probably take until tomorrow night just to get there. I suppose I could catch some sort of flight back, I reasoned. I have a little money in savings.

Then, without further hesitation, I went to my closet and grabbed my red backpack. I put a change of clothes in it, some water, a few snacks, and then told my husband and my youngest daughter, now a teen, that I was going to accompany Molly back home and that I would return sometime on Monday.

They both regarded me inquisitively. It's not every day that Mom announces that she's jetting off somewhere for the weekend.

I gave them a brief explanation and let them know that I would call them when I knew more.

When Molly's car pulled into my driveway, I opened the door and got in. "I'm going with you," I told her. And much to my astonishment, I heard no objections. Actually, there was no reply of any kind.

With brief spurts of small talk, we drove down the country back roads making our way toward Interstate 90 east. An hour later, we came to the entry ramp to the Interstate in North Bend and headed toward the pass. After about ten or fifteen minutes, Molly asked me to call her brother to give him my cell number.

"That way, he can call and keep me informed about Mom," she explained.

"Sure," I said, nodding understandingly.

She called out the number to her brother's phone and I dialed.

"Hi, is this John?"

"Yes," came the reply on the other end.

"This is Molly's friend, Pat. I am with her right now traveling up Interstate 90. She asked me to call you and give you the number to my cell phone so that you can keep in touch.

"Will you put Molly on?" he asked."

"Yes. Just a minute," I answered and turned to Molly, handing her the phone. "He wants to talk to you."

And that's when Molly learned about the passing of her mother.

Sensing this, I instantly motioned her to pull off to the side of the interstate and then switched seats with her. You can only imagine receiving news of the death of your mother while you're driving up a mountainous interstate at seventy miles an hour.

When we reached the top of the pass, Molly directed me to pull into the parking lot of the ski resort there, where she got out of the car sobbing and went off to come to grips with the reality of her loss. After about a half hour, she returned.

"I need to make this trip home alone," she said quietly. "I hope that you understand. I'll drive you back to your house."

"You don't have to do that, Molly," I said with compassion. I was concerned for her. "Let me make a couple of phone calls. I'm sure that I can find a ride back."

In reality, I hadn't a clue on whom I could impose to drive up to the top of Snoqualmie Pass to fetch me. As it was, I was well over an hour from home. But I thought that I could start with my neighbor and friend, Marianne, and if she was not able or willing to come, I would call my sixteen-year-old daughter, who had just obtained her driver's license. To expect her to drive by herself up the mountain would be pushing it.

The gods were on my side that day. When I called Marianne she told me that she was in Issaquah, less than a half hour away, finishing up a few errands and that she would be more than happy to come and pick me up. Bless her heart.

So I hugged Molly good-bye and sent her on her way, and in exactly twenty-five minutes, Marianne arrived to pick me up.

In the days to come, I received telephone calls at home from various friends of Molly's thanking me for being there with her on that sad day. All of them wanted to know what had prompted me to accompany her on that trip, and all I could tell them was the truth, that something or someone inside of me had urged me to do so. And so I had.

However, there is some happy news to report, too. A few years later, Molly received an unexpected phone call from a man with whom she was once acquainted back in her hometown. Actually, they had been romantically entangled, as the saying goes, in their college years but had parted ways some time ago. As it turned out, he was now in town for a business meeting of some sort. He wanted to know if she would consider having dinner with him that evening.

Being the forthright person that she was, Molly was honest and told him that she was leaving the next day for a trip back home to spend the summer with her father, but that perhaps they might hook up for dinner another time.

Short story—they were married a year later.

Since that time, I have lost both of my parents, as well as my very best friend from high school, who had suffered greatly from MS. I have come to realize that these personal losses can either frighten you into an inertia of dread of what lies ahead for us all, or they can give you a broader perspective about what life really is all about, how it all works, and has worked from the very beginning.

Or you can choose to live life following the wisdom and inspiration of my personal sage, Tom, who always says: "What the hell. I'm not going to worry about it."

Truly one of the most brilliant philosophers of our time.

12

Simply Grand

One of the most majestic views that I have ever beheld is at Grand Park, located in the Sunrise area of Mount Rainier National Park where Tom and I went hiking a few summers ago.

Generally, one can access Grand Park taking the trail from Sunrise, about fourteen miles round trip, but Tom knew of a shorter route via a hiker-trodden footpath by way of a fishing lake called Lake Eleanor.

So one gloriously sunny morning we headed toward Mount Rainier, making our way up a dirt road until Tom spotted the trailhead where we then began our hike. As is par for the course, we traveled up and down and through the forest, jabbering animatedly until at one point we began to notice that the closer we got to Lake Eleanor, the buggier it became. Specifically, I am referring to mosquitoes.

If there is one thing I can't stand, and there are a lot of things on my "can't stand" list, it is mosquitoes. They really make me nervous with all that ear buzzing and, of course, the surprise bite, if that's what you want to call it. Is the drilling of skin with the intention of sucking out blood really considered biting? Well, actually, yes if you are a referring to a vampire. Maybe we should not call them mosquitoes (little flies) but vampiritoes (little vampires.)

Onward toward the lake we went, and the mosquito population got thicker. Mind you, these were not your normal urban mosquitoes. These were giant, savage, and unrelenting mountain mosquitoes.

Even though we wore long hiking pants and long-sleeve shirts drenched with our "all natural" mosquito repellent, we were being swarmed, virtually eaten alive. Attaching themselves, not only to exposed skin like hands, foreheads, neck and ears, they were biting us through our clothes! Swarms had even affixed themselves to our backpacks, as if the packs were living, blood-filled canvas beings.

At one point, I started brandishing my hat about like an escaped lunatic but with no fruitful effect whatsoever. The horrid buggers just sat there on my hat staring me down, plotting where next to strike.

Then came the moment when Tom and I looked at each other and knew. We knew that it was time. It was time to bring out the big guns.

Deet!

Soon we came to and passed Lake Eleanor and, following the posted sign, took the turn toward Grand Park. We traveled through cool forests, over streams and brooks, and across beautiful meadows where Tom stopped to retrieve the flower book from his backpack to examine the many species of flora. Given that every time we stopped the mosquitoes continued to attack us as if we were slabs of raw meat, I continued hiking up the trail, allowing my long-legged husband to catch up.

Along the way, we were lucky enough to spot a couple of elk, which moved on soon enough, and we took pictures of hillsides covered with lovely avalanche lilies.

We also met other hikers, giving our salutations when passing. On one such occasion we were passed up by a fast, energetic group of six young people, looking to be about eighteen or nineteen years of age and dressed in tank tops, shorts, and tennis shoes. They stopped for a moment to inquire whether they were on the right path to Grand Park, and we assured them that they were. Tom and I glanced at each other with raised eyebrows. No protective clothing? No backpacks with food or water? Novices! We'll see.

I think the entire one-way hike was about three and a half miles, and it was after ascending a lengthy hill that we broke out into an expanse of the most beautiful meadow I had ever seen. Nature's carpet of wildflowers in purple, magenta, yellow, white blue, and red were scattered before us as far as the eye could see, with a snow-covered Mount Rainier standing proudly at the far end.

The view was stunning!

We continued to advance forward on a narrow, dirt footpath through the meadow, admiring nature's amazing bouquet, with Tom, once again, extracting his flower book to look up names of flowers that he would not remember two days later.

I used to tease Tom about that flower book. Years ago, when we were dating and hiked with the Mountaineers Singles Group—generally comprised of widowed or divorced adults over the age of forty-five—there were several outings on which I observed a lady or two hanging back from the group to join Tom in his floral research. Standing close, both heads peering into the book, I recognized that sweet voice and feigned botanical interest for what it was: keenly masked flirtatious intentions.

Please! I invented that move! Whenever I brought this to his attention, Tom would just chuckle and concur.

Wandering slowly along the path, we happened upon the group of young hikers once again, sitting on a log, but this time not appearing so jolly.

"Excuse me, sir." One of the fellows summoned Tom. "Do you have any insect repellent that you could share?"

We regarded the kids, who were now covered head to toe with red welts. Tom got out his DEET and handed it to them. They were understandably quite speedy to drench themselves with the insecticide, and then they thanked us profusely. We also gave them an unopened bag of trail mix for we sensed that they probably could use it about then. Once again, they expressed their gratitude.

After Tom and I had found an obliging log on which sit, we ate lunch and then decided to explore a bit further down the open trail. With his flower book in hand, Tom engaged in examining every petal, every stem, and every leaf. Soon we happened upon a woman who also had paused on her tour to consult her flower book. And so, the two botany enthusiasts united to enthusiastically engage in flower talk, identifying this one and that one, while I moseyed patiently.

After a while, my patient mosey pooped out, and I quietly told Tom that I was going to start heading back down the meadow path toward where we had entered. He said that he wouldn't be long and that he would catch up directly. So I strolled leisurely, taking in the sunshine and enjoying the clean, crisp air. But it wasn't long before something caught my ear, something off in the brush to my right.

I stopped walking and listened. I heard the noise again. It sounded like a growl coming from those trees over yonder.

I knew that we were in bear country, but I tried not to panic. My friend, Pam, and her husband had once encountered a bear eating berries on a trail near here. She told me that they had to wait quietly for over an hour until the bear ambled off, allowing them to move on. Even though the bear hadn't paid much attention to them, they admitted to having been just a shade under petrified.

Ever so nonchalantly, I turned around and walked briskly back to where I had left Tom and the woman, who were still debating whether what they were looking at was a *Wellblowmedown stragulatus* or *Sippysunrise*.

"I heard a growl over there," I announced animatedly to Tom when I had reached him and the woman. "Right over there." I pointed to the small grove of trees. "I think it might be a bear." It took all of my will power not to project too much hysteria. "I could hear it clearly from the trail."

"From that bunch of trees over there?" the woman asked, calmly looking up from her book and pointing in said direction.

"Yes," I answered excitedly.

"Oh," she said. "That's my husband." She went on to explain. "Nearly every weekend during the summer we come up here to Grand Park. I come to look at flowers and plants, while he comes to take a nap. That's him, over there"—she pointed—"zipped up in his sleeping bag. He snores like a snorting bull moose."

Well, that was a relief. Unusual, but still a relief.

Tom told me the story of a hike he once took with his son, Dan. These two men, when together, tend to combine their adventurous energies and become extremists. On one particularly sunny day, they traveled from the trailhead, up and through Grand Park continuing on a distance over the ridge and through a valley for several additional hours. As is always the case, the return trip seemed to take infinitely longer than the arrival trip, resulting in a reentrance through Grand Park at dusk with still a couple of hiking hours to go.

Making their careful way through the large meadow, much to their surprise, Tom and Dan witnessed a small caravan of various hikers coming up the trail and into Grand Park.

"What gives?" The two looked at each other wondering why so many people would be ascending the trail and emerging from the woods this late in the day. Various people arrived alone, while others came with family and friends. They carried cameras and tripods, blankets, baskets of food, and thermoses of hot drinks. It was like a family reunion had been scheduled for midnight.

Tom and Dan paused in their tracks for a moment and took stock. Then it dawned on them. They looked up into the dim sky to see the beginning of a full moon and realized that such nights were a photographer's delight. When the sun sets and the full moon dominates, the silhouette of Mount Rainier is awe inspiring, or so I am told.

I wish I could report that Tom and Dan stayed at the park to witness this soul-stirring event, but having traveled nearly eighteen miles, they were not only tired but also hungry, and so they continued toward the trailhead. Now, had I been there, I might have decided to stay if it weren't for the, you know, bears.

Returning to the adventures of Tom and Pat, and before I lose you, I can tell you that our summer hike to Grand Park turned out to be very profitable. Oh sure, the monster vampire mosquitoes might have made the experience a living hell, but the view at Grand Park was nothing short of glorious, right? And so what if we spent hours slipping through mud and muck, climbing over impossibly huge logs and rocks and, in general, compromising the integrity of our antiquated muscles and ligaments, while remaining cautious enough to avert an unexpected catastrophe that might land us on the evening news.

Think of the crisp fresh air, the quiet of the forest, and the exquisite freedom to explore nature at will...the ten-dollar bill that I spotted under a bush along the path while making my tenuous way back to the car.

"What did you say?" you ask. Yes siree, Bob, a ten-dollar bill, all folded up and waiting for me to come along to discover it, which, thanks to my ever-so-keen eyes, I did.

Ah, nature! Don't you just love it?

13

Out One Door and in Another

id you know that wet towels dry in less than an hour in Utah as compared to the day or two it requires to do the same in the Northwest? I learned that on our camping excursion to the Southwest.

Whenever my daughters get fed up with the cold, rainy weather of home, they just ask Tom and me to go on vacation. We have told them that, whenever we leave town, it is always unseasonably cold and/or rainy at our planned destination, all the while unseasonably sunny and warm here at home. And that is exactly how it was when Tom and I headed south toward the canyon lands of Utah and Colorado.

We planned our trip for the end of April that year, enthusiastically packing, along with our hiking clothes and boots, several pair of shorts, five or six tank tops, our sunhats, sunglasses, and plenty of sunscreen. We didn't want to come back too sunburned, you know, just pleasantly tanned.

I know what you're going to say. A tan is very damaging to the skin as well. Sheesh! Can't even enjoy a good, old-fashioned, tan any more. I don't know about you, but just the thought of the warm sun on my skin makes me giddy.

Two weeks was all I could afford to be gone from work. At that time, I was employed at a small local hospital, where I worked in the community relations department, and a new director had just come on board. Being gone for more than two weeks would have made things difficult for her, being new and all.

So late one Friday afternoon, Tom rolled into the parking lot of the hospital in his truck with travel trailer in tow, and we headed out, bound for the freedom of the open road. We spent our first night near Pendleton, Oregon, where after having a simple dinner, we both fell into an exhausted sleep. That freedom of the open road, however, came to an abrupt end at five the next morning. That's right, five o'clock in the morning, when Tom woke me up telling me that we had to get going in order to stay "on schedule."

"I'm on vacation!" I growled, but my resistance was futile. We were packed up and headed down the road in less than an hour, me semicomatose. Alas, I don't drink coffee.

It was a mere hour after takeoff that my husband realized that he had left the keys to the camper on the picnic table back at the campground. We would have to turn around and go back.

I just looked at him but didn't say a word. It would have been cruel to mention that this would mean we would now be two hours behind "schedule." Fun, yes in a touché kind of way, but I resisted. I wasn't feeling as sharp at that hour of the morning as I would have been at that same hour of the evening.

Nevertheless, we were soon back on course in no time and heading southeast to the canyons of the Southwest. Our travels took us to Arches National Park, camping along the Colorado River and Hovenweep, a wonderfully quiet place where we camped amid ancient cliff-dweller ruins, which included signs reminding us to pay attention, while exploring, as to where we placed our hands. Apparently, there are rattlesnakes in the Southwest.

We traveled east to Mesa Verde, Colorado, which brought a couple inches of snow along with fifty-plus elementary school children to accompany us on the tour through the Anasazi ruins there.

The panoramic Monument Valley was amazing, but it did give me pause to recall Forrest Gump and his notorious "I just felt like running," statement, soon to be followed with the equally powerful "I think I'll go home now." I was starting to feel the same way about then, not the part about feeling like running, but about going home. We were only halfway through our planned itinerary, but my back end was already starting to feel like concrete.

We traveled up the white-knuckle Moki (Mokee) Dugway, a narrow, switchback road carved into the face of a cliff edge and also not recommended for trailers and RVs but on Tom's "We'll be OK" route.

We put down anchor at Bridges National Monument for a day and then moved on to Capital Reef and more cold and rain. The locals had been telling us all along that this was the coldest, wettest spring they could remember, but that did not surprise us. For this camping duo, just starting up the truck was the white man's rain dance.

No one can deny that the colors of the Capital Reef are spectacular: vivid oranges, pinks, and yellows, depending on the lighting. I came to understand by the posted signs that flash floods could be an issue, though, and thus caution was advised.

After our overnight stay, we were on to our final destination, Bryce Canyon. I was not prepared for Bryce Canyon. Talk about impressive! After climbing the road up and up and up, we arrived at one of the most stunning spots on earth.

The canyon presented us with a dazzling burst of brilliant orange, red, and pink and was filled with thousands of orange hoodoos, those spire-like formations you see in the tour books about the Southwest. We saw green pine trees, along with the usual wildlife that tourists expect to see: deer, squirrels, and chipmunks.

We spent a day hiking down through the canyon, exploring the nooks, crannies, valleys, and ledges. About an hour into our trek, we heard the rumble of thunder and looked out to see streaks of lightning in the distance and dark clouds headed our way.

I quickly recalled the signs at the parking lot advising visitors to avoid being out on high spots during lightning. Duh! I also remembered from my school days science class that lightning tends to strike the tallest things in its path. I looked around and, frankly, the tallest thing nearest to me was Tom.

"You can dawdle if you want," I told him. "I'm making a beeline back to the truck!"

And with that, I left Tom in my orange dust. He brought up a slow rear, droning on about how it would be OK and there was nothing to worry about, and so forth. Tom still gives me grief about abandoning him, but hey, every woman for herself! He also likes to tell people that he'd never seen me move so fast in all his life.

It wasn't, however, the first time we'd found ourselves at a high elevation when stormy weather blew through. We were in Coeur d'Alene, Idaho, visiting family and took a walk up the town's infamous Tubbs Hill. It is a short, pleasant hike up a hill in the downtown area along Lake Coeur d'Alene, popular among locals and tourists alike. We found ourselves walking along the top ridge when a thunderstorm rolled in.

In the advent of lightning, we began to look around for some type of cover, like a picnic shelter or small cave, but we found nothing. The trail was completely exposed. Given our options, we marched quickly through the pelting rain, cringing with the arrival of every bolt of lightning and rumble of thunder.

The storm intensified while we hurried down the trail, when we happened upon a port-a-potty. Tom looked at me, and I at him.

"No way!" I said. But the next crack of lightning hit close enough to send us both flying into the smelly, plastic structure where we remained until the storm passed.

After returning to his brother's house, Tom shared with all those present that it was one of the most romantic moments he'd ever experienced. The big tease.

Back at Bryce Canyon, we got back to the parking lot before the storm hit. Actually, it had bypassed us altogether. Nary a drop of rain had moistened our brows. Much ado about nothing, as usual. We were sweaty, however, given the speed of our elevation gain out of the canyon, and covered with orange dust from head to toe.

When we were getting into our truck and were about to leave the parking lot to head back to the campgrounds, we spotted a tour bus pulling in, one of many, actually. The occupants of this particular bus were Japanese tourists.

Now, far be it for me to generalize, but in my experience, I have found Japanese tourists to be very neat and clean people. From head to toe, they present themselves impeccably. I always feel so dowdy and ill kept when I'm in the presence of a Japanese tourist. This is not a distasteful quality—au contraire. I wish I had inherited even a minute amount of that neatness gene. It's all I can do to wash my face, comb my morning bed head, and choose a top that goes reasonably well with my bottoms—that is, white T-shirt and blue jeans.

You can imagine my anxiety (it doesn't take much, as you know) when I spotted the group of tourists, now headed down the same path that we had just recently ascended, in their clean, cotton shirts and pants, sun hats, and ever-so-brilliantly-white canvas shoes.

"Oh no," I groaned under my breath. "Do you suppose they have any idea that the orange-colored soil covering this entire canyon will, more than certainly, change the color of those spanking-white shoes forever? It will never come out."

"Well," Tom replied, "perhaps it'll make for a great Southwest souvenir."

At any rate, we didn't hang around to see, and so began our way back to the campgrounds. After we made dinner, Tom had a couple glasses of red wine and then tried to talk me into driving the truck out to a point well known for its sunset. He is very responsible when it comes to alcohol, but I had never driven a truck in my life and wasn't about to give it a try then.

Tom, however, is a notoriously pushy fellow. "Come on; it's easy. It's no different from driving a car," he encouraged.

"I could see it if we were going to an isolated parking lot somewhere in the flat lands to practice new driving skills," I reasoned, "but we are in a national park in the mountains, at a very high elevation." I envisioned myself behind the wheel of the pickup, neck craned, struggling to see out the windshield as we plunged hundreds of feet over a cliff to our final resting place next to a chipmunk or two and some rusty-looking sneakers.

"Besides, I'm tired and going to find the shower." I'll bet that you guessed that it was the "cranky" hour. Traveling can sure wear you out.

After gathering up the usual public showering paraphernalia for some reason, Tom preferred that we avoid using our camper's shower on that trip—I headed off to the building where the showers were.

Now this was my kind of showering place! Clean and spacious, it had a zillion immaculate shower stalls from which to choose. Plus, and this was the best part of all, I had the whole place to myself. Per usual, I had timed it all just right, waiting until everyone had already showered and were now sitting all cozy around their campfires.

So humming myself into a rapture in anticipation of the warm shower to come, I chose my stall—one about midway down the aisle. I proceeded to follow my customary routine: placing the soap and shampoo over here, my glasses out of the way over there, the towel on a hook, and my flip-flops just beyond reach of water, and so forth. I then turned on the warm water to full throttle to initiate said rapture.

It hadn't even been a minute before I heard someone come in to use the toilet. That figures, but no problem...yet. I continued to go about my own business of showering, when I heard the person leave the stall, run the faucet, run the hand dryer, turn off the lights, and go out the door.

Good Lord, it was pitch black in there! In a flash, I shouted, "I'm in here. Turn the lights back on, please!"

But the door slammed shut, and no one came back in. Or at least I hoped that no one had come back in. All sorts of things began to run through my head. Was the person still in there? Had she or he planned this? Was the person waiting for me? Was this *Psycho II*?

I was scared. It was so dark that I could not see a thing. Nothing! I reached in front of me, found the knob for the water, and turned it off. I put my arms out in search of my towel, which I eventually located and wrapped around myself. Carefully, taking a few steps to the left and then to the right, I was able to find my flip-flops and ease into them.

I wasn't sure what to do next. When I'd entered the bathroom, I hadn't really paid any attention to the layout of the place. I knew that there were windows up high by the ceiling, but because it was nighttime, no light was coming in. I knew that the door was somewhere down to my left, but I really didn't know how far.

Carefully, so as not to slip and tumble on the wet floor, I found the latch and opened my door. When I was out of the stall, I turned to my left and, using my left hand, began to follow the row of stalls. As all of the doors were partially open, I advanced cautiously.

Edging my way forward, I kept my right hand straight out in front of me, not only to avoid running into anything, but to avoid a surprise of any kind. Slowly, I shuffled my way forward, shaking like a leaf.

In what seemed like an eternity, I sensed that I had passed the final stall. My left foot kicked some plastic thing on the floor. My hand slipped from the edge of the last stall to the wall and miraculously, my fingers found the light switch.

Immediately, I flipped on the light and looked around. From what I could see, there was no one else in there. From scared to pissed in zero point two, I flew in a fury out the door in my towel, flip-flops, and wet hair and headed straight to the front desk in the lobby.

I began to rage at the poor fellow at the desk, who had that "yikes!" expression on his face, giving him every incensed detail of my traumatic experience. Quickly, and while I stood there drip-drying on the carpet, he raced into the ladies shower room and returned shortly after, assuring me that he had inspected it thoroughly and that it was safe for me to return to finish my shower.

Ha! As if I would shower now!

He had in his hand the plastic cover, which previously had been over the light switch to keep it from being turned off. He shook his head relating that he couldn't imagine how anyone could have removed the cover from the wall, as it had been screwed on.

My highly keen intuition told me that that the culprit was a brat between the age of twelve and sixteen. However, when you're cold, wet, and dripping in front of a young man who, before that moment, had been a complete stranger—and a cute one at that—all rationality goes out the door...right after the brat before it. All right, the alleged brat.

Soon enough, our abbreviated tour of the Southwest ended, and we headed for home.

The following Monday, I returned to work only to find out that I had been laid off. The community relations department existed no more, and a new marketing department had been established. Since I had absolutely no marketing experience, I received the boot.

I was devastated. My good friend, who was the executive assistant to the CEO, later told me that it was the hardest confidentiality she'd ever had to keep.

After I received the news, I was told that I could go home. I sat in my car in the parking lot of the hospital for a while, sobbing. Then I called Tom.

At the time, Tom was on a quick trip to Coeur d'Alene to visit his mother. When he answered the phone, I couldn't speak, just bawl. Because of his keen sense of the state I was in, Tom immediately left Idaho for home, arriving late that night, but early enough to console me into the wee hours of the morning. He assured me that, even though it was devastating news, there isn't a soul on earth who doesn't go through this sooner or later.

Not to worry, though, because as the saying goes, "When one door closes, another opens." Sort of makes me want to barf, but in this case it landed me in the technology department of Everett Public School, where I worked with the best staff on earth for six years, before retiring.

In 2011, I came across a quote by MIT THINK founder, Di Ye. She asks, "What can be more rewarding and joyful than encountering pleasant surprises along a challenging path, finding hidden treasures after you've struggled and sweated, and arriving at a place you never dared to dream about through a journey created all on your own?"

Hell, I don't think any of that applies to me, but it sounds pretty cool, doesn't it?

14

The Art of Survival

One afternoon, I walked into my living room and, glancing out the front window, spotted a man out on our front lawn. He was wearing a white T-shirt so full of holes that it looked like it had been used for target practice, a pair of bloomer shorts, the kind with pleats that were fashionable in the '80s, and barn boots. He was frozen in place, staring down at the ground with a pistol in his hand.

Yep, you guessed it. It was Tom.

I opened the window. "What are you doing?" I asked with a "what now?" tone.

"I'm going to get that mole if it's the last thing I do," was his battle cry. Nary an eye did he shift from the targeted pile of dirt.

I shook my head and shut the window. I thought he was supposed to be cleaning the garage that day. Oh—wait a minute. That was in my fantasy.

Actually, he was supposed to be packing for our trip to his family's cabin. You remember—the rustic one that I had found so romantic in the beginning...until the charm wore off and reality set it. We were going for some last-chance spring skiing at Crystal Mountain. Well, Tom was going to ski. I was going for what would be the final acrobatics of my abbreviated skiing career.

It wasn't even a very big hill. In fact, it wasn't a hill at all. It was more like a softly slanted driveway planted near the beginning path of the ski lift. I had been down it several times before, ho-humming along, but I was never quite ready for the big times. On that particular day, and after a couple of effortless runs, Tom decided that I needed to perfect my "form." Apparently, survival was not the goal of skiing at all. Maneuvers to enhance the style of the experience were called for.

With Tutor Tom at the helm, it went something like this:

"Bend your knees. No, not that much. Like this (demonstration.) Now, keep your arms relaxed in front of you. Grip your poles lightly. Put all your weight on the middle of the skis. Don't lean forward. Don't lean backward. Relax your shoulders. For smoother turns—in this case, traversing an area the size of a child's wading pool—squat slightly into the turn and then pop back up as you begin your turn in the opposite direction; then down, then up..."

Next came the most important instructional piece of all: "If you feel yourself getting into the backseat"—translation, about to fall on your ass—"throw your arms out in front of you to right yourself. Got it?"

Sure. Whatever.

The plan was for me to practice my new "form" on this very short, but steep part of the beginner's hill, which I appraised as easy-peasy and thus, with just the tiniest bit of ski swagger, pushed off and headed forth down the slope.

Within seconds of takeoff, I knew that I was in deep doo-doo. I was headed for the dreaded backseat! As instructed, and reacting quickly, I pushed my arms out in front of me, thus precipitating one grandiose alpine cartwheel, tumbling over and over and over, coming to an eventual halt in a tangled pile near the bottom. I sensed that one of my skis had not released and that my left knee had contorted in a direction never meant for any human body part. The pain was excruciating.

"Are you all right?" Tom came quickly skiing toward me.

In an effort to conceal any further public humiliation, I tried not to cry. "I cannot tell you," I told him calmly, "how badly I have hurt myself."

Tom helped release the rogue ski. "Well, get up," he ordered.

I gave him a look that said, *Please tell me that you didn't just say that.*

He looked at me and reacted quickly to save himself. "Can you get up?"

"No."

He bent down and went about gentling untwining my legs and helping me to my feet. It took some doing to get my booted feet locked back into the skis, given that my left knee was by then the size of a cantaloupe.

"Now, here is how you should proceed back down," my ski guru—husband advised. "Just go straight. Don't do any turns. Just go straight until you reach the bottom." And with that, he turned and headed down the slope ahead of me.

"OK," I mumbled, as if I could execute even the simplest of turns at that point. It was all I could do to stand up. I was somewhat miffed that he didn't escort me, but given that the rest of the course was nearly as flat as most of the cakes that I bake, I started back down the slope, hoping that I would not lose my balance, which I didn't.

Now here is the part that, for me, was truly dumbfounding. When I reached the end of the run, I looked over to my right to see Tom standing at the entrance to the ski lift.

"Well, come on," he shouted. "Where're you going?"

That was the moment I realized that, beyond any reasonable doubt, the man I had married lived in his own world. Moles, skis, imaginary friends...his own world, I tell you.

I blew right past him, well not blew exactly, more like glided smoothly, and looking directly forward, coasted to the concessions where I ordered up a hot chocolate and a bag of ice.

And that's when I turned my back on alpine self-annihilation. That's when I voted for survival of the not-so-fittest. That's when I hung up my skis for good. Actually, they were given to Tom's daughter-in-law, which turned out to be a timely donation, since her skis had recently been, shall we say, erroneously removed from a ski rack during a recent outing.

In any case, I was free, free, free!

⟶ ⟶

Lying awake up in the loft that night, having been awoken by the crashing of clumps of snow falling from the trees onto the tin roof, I reviewed the day's adventures and thought about what a beautiful skier Tom was. Very smooth and graceful in his turns, Tom was confident but not careless. I marveled at how one person could have such a perfect sense of balance while another—and I'm not naming names here, but she's the same one that took up ice skating on her lunch break and ended up body-surfing across the ice—lacks this graceful sense of equilibrium.

Side note: here is some helpful information for those females over the age of fifty-five who may decide to take up ice skating for exercise: the "girls" are of no use to you if you find yourself in a free-fall forward, as one heads east, while the other heads west, leaving your rib cage as your only line of defense. On a positive note, at least you can ice your injuries right away.

I would like to add here, however, that Tom does have issues with what I refer to as "ski feet." This is a syndrome consisting of bunions, bone spurs, blackened toenails, flattened soles, and a multitude of other painful conditions resulting from encasing one's feet in circulation-prohibiting, shin-compressing, ankle-immobilizing, toe-smashing, rigid plastic mobile tombs, popularly referred to as ski boots.

He goes to his podiatrist on a regular basis, and on a recent visit at which I had accompanied him, during the doctor's examination of Tom's feet, I asked the fellow why they couldn't just use collagen injections on people's feet, like they do their faces, filling in the flattened pads, toes, ankles, and so forth. I didn't hear any type of reply, which one might deduce was due to the intense concentration of the examination of Tom's feet by the podiatrist. Personally, I think the good doctor had taken the idea in and was quietly but excitedly planning his early retirement based on this absolutely ingenious podiatric-transforming idea of mine.

But I've gone off track here. Now where was I? Oh yes...Tom's graceful turns, sense of balance, blah, blah...oh, now I remember. I was lying
awake in the loft doing a lot of thinking that night about this and that
and the other—sleep does not often come quickly to a postmenopausal
woman—and began to contemplate a notion that I had recently read in
Eckhart Tolle's *The Power of Now.*

This spiritual teacher infers that love, for most of us, is nothing
more than an addictive clinging. I have spent a considerable amount of
time pondering in depth this light of a different color. Well, perhaps
not a considerable amount of time, but I did mull it over once or twice
before deciding to put this radical concept before Tom that night.

"You know," I whispered to him just as he was on the verge of
dosing off, "in the book that I've been reading, the author, Eckhart
Tolle, explains that love, as most of us know it, can be nothing more
than an addictive clinging." To which the sweet man replied without
missing a lullaby beat, "Probably so," and promptly fell into a deep
slumber.

From consciousness to unconsciousness in zero point two.

One thing that drives me crazy is when Tom gets up on our roof to clean
it and the gutters. I mean, the man is not exactly a spring rooster, although he thinks that he is. I have seen him climb up ladders, sometimes
employing the top rung even though the ladder's warning sticker advises
against that, to climb to the roof in the pouring rain.

I had asked him many times to please not go up on the roof while
I was not at home, but it was like telling him to refrain from wearing
baggy sweats, the green ones with elastic around the ankles, when he
goes to town to the bank. In one ear and out the other.

So one afternoon, when calling him from work, I found that I had
no choice but to use tough love on him:

Me: "What are you doing?"

Him: "I'm up cleaning off the roof."

Me: "I don't like it when you're on the roof when I'm at work, Tom. That makes it tough on me."

Him: "It needs to be done. Why does it make it tough on you?"

Me: "It creates a bit of a dilemma."

Him: "What do you mean? How does it create a dilemma for you?"

Me: "Well, if I come home from work to find you splat on the ground, deader than our phones during a windstorm, I won't know if I should lament, 'Oh no! Oh no!' or, given the status of your life insurance policy, I should shout, 'Yes!'"

Him: "You're mean."

Me: "Then please don't go up on the roof when I'm not home!"

～ ～

Given that he has almost five acres of rain forest to play with, Tom also likes to take down his own dead trees. In this case, however, he does comply with my request to please wait until I'm at home before he starts his lumberjack activity.

On one particular day, I had just arrived home from work when he ran up and told me that he was about to take down a dead tree. He pointed out, proudly, that he had waited until I had come home before starting. Then he outlined the plan for me.

"When you hear the chain saw start up, come out onto the back deck," he instructed. "After the tree comes down, I'll yell up to you that everything's OK."

"Got it," I said.

So as planned, when I heard the chainsaw start up, I scooted outside and stood on the deck, peering in the direction of his project. After a few minutes, I heard the tree crash down and then the chainsaw revert to idle. I waited, but there was no "OK" signal from Tom.

"Tom?" I shouted.

No response.

I shouted again, "Tom?"

Nothing. Just the idling of the chainsaw's motor.

Then I heard our neighbor, Dave, yell out from his yard across the street. "Tom?"

Still no response. Oh no!

I flew back into the house from the deck and out the front door running in my bare feet across the lawn toward our grove of trees, when to my relief out from the forest walked Tom...with earplugs in his ears.

"That son of a gun didn't fall exactly right," he explained, "and got snagged up in another tree."

"You were supposed to yell to me that you were all right. You scared me half to death!" I scolded.

"What?" Then he took his earplugs out. "Oh, sorry. What did you say?"

And you wonder why I'm gray...well, at the roots anyway.

⚊ ⚊

Here in the Northwest, nothing brings fear to my heart like a windstorm, and we get a fair share of windstorms. Because we are blessed with lots and lots of very tall trees—I mean trees that are in excess of 150 feet—it is not unusual to lose our power when windstorms visit. What's more, when we lose power, it always means that one or more neighborhood trees have come down. Our windstorms are not just unnerving, but they can be downright deadly, with trees sometimes falling across roads of traffic and crashing through homes.

Recently, after one particularly strong windstorm, a friend of Tom's related to him the following story. As an insurance agent, he had been called out to investigate a claim of damage to a client's home. In the process of assessing the damage, the owners of the house took him out to see a tree that had fallen on their property. Although the fallen tree had nothing to do with the home's storm damage, there was something of interest.

As the story goes, over the past couple of years, the owners had been keeping their eyes on the goings on of a bald eagle's nest perched high at the top of one of their cottonwood trees. The day after the windstorm, they found that the cottonwood had not survived the storm's destruc-tion, and the couple went to investigate.

Near the top end of the downed tree, they located the now vacant eagle's nest. And entangled in the nest they noticed something shiny ly-ing amid the debris. It was a small pet's collar. Soon enough, they came upon another pet collar, and then another, and still another.

Incredibly, in all, the owners had counted almost eighty pet collars!

Have your hands flown to your cheeks now in horror? Poor little things! Who can deny their sympathy for all of the desperate pet owners who have gone looking for their little Fluffy or posted pictures of their Muffin on utilities poles with the words "Lost" or "Have you seen me?"

Yes, we all understand that it's part of the nature of things, but if a pet has ever been a member of your family, you know that it is a devastat-ing reality to accept, and still sad even if you've never had a pet.

Now going back to the very beginning of this chapter, do you re-member Tom's nemesis, the mole? In the end, the dog got it.

Such is life. Like trying to nudge your husband into cleaning the garage, it is what it is.

15

Dancing with Grizzlies

A while back, my eldest daughter and her husband vacationed in Banff National Park in Alberta, Canada. They shared with us some of the beautiful photos that they had taken, and I, in awe of the splendor of the region, made a quiet comment to myself, something like, "That is so beautiful! I wouldn't mind seeing that."

That tentative, itsy-bitsy idea of a short car trip to visit Banff sometime, perhaps one of these days, was—in no time at all—picked up by my husband, interpreted, and morphed into a nine-day camping excursion to Banff National Park.

I swear I don't know how I allow myself to get pulled into these situations. Although I love being in nature, I really don't care for camping that much. It's a lot of work, not to mention the inconveniences for something that is meant to be relaxing.

Well, what can I say? I have a lifelong history of being a people pleaser, often doing what I really don't want to do. That effort is then usually followed up with an era of endless whining about that which I didn't want to do in the first place, thereby driving the target of my original loving intention quite mad. I think those in the field of psychology call it passive-aggressive behavior. Whatever. I'm a Scorpio. Enough said.

So after Tom had created the itinerary and made the campground reservations, we packed up the entire house and transplanted it into the travel trailer, leaving the uncharacteristic summer heat of Washington behind and headed to Canada.

Since Tom was unable to secure a campsite reservation for us at Banff National Park, our final destination was Lake Louise, about an hour's drive outside of Banff. After two full days of traveling and after my feet, legs, and behind had all fallen into a forty-eight-hour coma, we arrived at our destination.

When we checked in at the park, we were given our site assignment, a map of the campgrounds, and a pamphlet on bears—specifically black and grizzly bears. We were also advised that there had been a grizzly bear sighting in the campground just fifteen minutes prior to our arrival, so we should be sure to keep all food inside the trailer or locked in the truck.

What the...! Say what?

Apparently, not only is Lake Louise home to a large population of bears, it is one of the few major hubs for grizzly sows and their cubs. Oh great!

The pamphlets that park staff gave to us provided essential information regarding how to avoid attracting bears to our campsite; the necessity of keeping all food safely locked inside a vehicle; being aware of our surroundings; not walking, hiking, or biking alone; and the importance of making noise when walking about. The pamphlets also explained the safety in numbers (four or more people), what to do if you come upon a bear, what to do if attacked by a bear, and how to say bye-bye to your hubby and hitch a ride back home with Justin, Jeremy, and Jenny in their yellow VW van with a kayak on top.

After reading all of the ever-so-urgent information provided in the pamphlets, and without the slightest of hesitation, I made it absolutely clear to my husband that I do not—and will not—hike in the land of grizzlies.

Tom's initial move was the ol' puppy dog frown, but he soon regained his he-man composure and launched in to his, "Aw, come on; it's nothing," persuasion front. But I stood fast like a wrought iron fence grounded in concrete. I was unmovable.

I do not hike with grizzlies! Don't hike, don't polka, don't hopscotch, and don't arm wrestle with grizzlies.

Frankly, I don't hike with rattlesnakes either, but that's another story.

Banff National Park was, without a doubt, the most beautiful place I had ever been to. As luck would have it, the weather during our visit was cold and off-and-on rainy, and—given my stance on the local wildlife—that limited our options to road explorations of well-known tourist attractions. We visited glaciers (Tom's favorite); pristine blue-green lakes, rivers, and waterfalls (my favorite); majestic mountain peaks (both of our favorites); and the town of Banff, a nice, yet typical, spot for tourists to eat, drink, and be merry.

Oddly, the most fascinating thing I found about the town of Banff had nothing to do with the beauty of the natural surroundings and everything to do with the crosswalks in the downtown area. Now, perhaps you also have this crosswalk configuration in your community, but I'd never experienced such a thing.

The crosswalks work like this: taking turns, cars go first in one direction, then the cross direction traffic goes, then the left-hand turns, and so forth. Then, after all the cars have had their turns, the pedestrian have theirs. All pedestrians cross the intersection at the same time... this way, that way, kitty-cornered. They have the entire intersection to themselves.

It was so fun! I laughed every time we got to cross the street and all of the people from all four corners met in the middle of the intersection, dodging left and right and every which way. Personally, I went out of my way to jaywalk as much as possible. I know, I know...I'm such a rebel.

Yes, we did see a bit of wildlife during our visit: one elk, one moose, two mountain goats, and one grizzly bear. Just as in Yellowstone, one can usually tell where the wildlife is by the presence of a multitude of cars pulled over to the side of the road. Makes no matter if it is a side road, highway, or interstate; the tourists must see their quota of wildlife before returning to their own wild lives.

After two days on the road getting to our campsite at Lake Louise and three days of traveling to the most popular tourist attractions, Tom, who is a very high-energy man, was itching to expend some of that energy out on the open, albeit ursidae-rambling, trail. So with my blessing and a stern reminder to hike where others were hiking, to be aware of his surroundings, to keep his bear (pepper) spray on him and at the ready, and above all, not to overdo it as he was the designated driver for our return trip home the next day, he packed his lunch and was off, locking the trailer door behind him as I climbed into a much-needed but water-stingy shower.

After showering, I, deciding to tidy up the camper a bit, launched into Susie homemaker mode, making the bed, washing the breakfast dishes, cleaning the bathroom, and stringing up a rope of wet towels, which hadn't dried out since our arrival.

Given that we were in a wilderness environment, I also decided to shake the wilderness out of the small throw rug by the door and sweep. Easy enough, right? But when I picked up the rug and went to open the door, the door would not budge.

The thing must be locked, I thought. Oh right. Tom, knowing that I was headed into the shower, locked it on his way out. I fumbled for the red lock-unlock switch near the door handle with the intention of moving it to the unlock position, but no dice. It wouldn't give. I tried every which way, even doing the hokey-pokey and turning all about, but the lock would not budge, nor would the door's latch.

Here I was alone in the quiet, isolated (except for the bears,) wilderness with nary a soul around, with the other campers off on their various daily vacation excursions, and I could not get out of my camper. I was locked in.

Now, I am a reasonably intelligent woman. What was the big deal? I know that in a real emergency, I could knock out one of the screens and crawl out through a window. In fact, I think that the window next to the bed is an emergency escape window. But there was something about being locked in that just set me on edge.

I didn't really need out. In fact, being inside was the exact place I wanted to be while alone in the wilderness, in a mountain forest that may or may not produce a bear at any moment. I had planned to put my feet up, relax, and do some reading. But I needed to be able to go outside when and if I wanted to, right? After all, it hadn't been my plan to confine myself to the camper the entire day.

I have to confess, however, that it was the "not being able to" that had me rattled.

I kept working at the door latch and lock with no success. Finally, I decided to pull open the window closest to the door, slide back the screen and stick my head out to assess the situation. I thought about using a broom handle or a wire wiener-roasting stick to poke at the outside door handle, but eventually figured that if the lock was the issue, this maneuver would not be the least bit helpful, not to mention being imbecilic.

As the minutes ticked along, for some unfathomable reason, I started to feel increasingly more anxious, something close to suffocating. I sat at the open window hoping that one of those park rangers would drive by. Then, I could hand the ranger my set of keys and ask him or her to try to open my door. But all was quiet with nary a ranger in sight.

To make a long and tedious story short, after about an hour, I spotted a lone woman emerge from a trailer three sites down. She walked back to her pickup truck to retrieve something, and although I felt incredibly foolish, I called to her through my open window.

"Excuse me," I called. "Could you help me?"

And without the slightest hesitation, she responded, "Sure," and made her way through the brush to my trailer.

I explained to her my predicament and then handed her my trailer keys. She easily unlocked the door and pulled it open.

"Thank you so much!" I said with relief. I also felt very silly. "I realize that in case of an emergency, I could have simply crawled out through the window, but..."

"I understand," she said matter-of-factly but kindly. "You start to feel claustrophobic."

"Exactly." I nodded. "Thank you."

And with that she returned to her campsite. I never saw her again.

Obviously, when Tom returned from his hike, earlier than expected and much to my relief, he got an earful of the day's drama. And of course the feedback I received was full of manly wisdom with, "You've just got to do this and that and then turn it this way," and so forth.

"You go inside," I commanded, feeling the irritation beginning to rise in me. "I'll lock you in. Then you try to get out."

"OK," he said confidently, climbing into the trailer.

I closed the door and locked it from the outside. "OK, open it," I directed him. (See, I said "directed" not "commanded" this time. Nicer touch, hey?)

And much to Tom's astonishment, he found himself in the same quandary that I had experienced earlier. I was ever so slightly tempted to keep him locked in there for an itsy-bitsy while longer, but the temptation passed quickly enough, as the situation didn't really warrant a payback, even though I admit that my orneriness was starting to kick into high gear.

Besides, that would leave him inside, warm and cozy with a hot dinner, and me outside, cold and damp and potentially some grizzly's dinner.

I'm no fool. I unlocked the door.

Hold on, Boo Boo. I'm a comin'!*

P.S. A friend of mine recently e-mailed me a link advising of the recall of said trailer locks.

*Quoted from cartoon character Yogi Bear

16

Shoe Tree

iking down the trail toward Berkley Camp at Mount Rainier on a fine summer day, we came upon a young family—dad, mom, and two kids, a boy and a girl—who were backpacking out. The family appeared a tad weary; the kids, who looked to be about eight and ten years old, looking absolutely miserable and were covered with welts from head to toe.

We stopped to chat with them, and in no time Tom had managed to weasel out every little tidbit of information about them. He's an awfully friendly, curious sort, you know.

They hailed from Canada and had been on a walkabout for about two weeks.

"This is the last leg of our hike through Washington State," the mom told us. "Then we are headed to Sunriver, Oregon."

"Sunriver!" I exclaimed wholeheartedly, trying my best to be genuinely friendly, like Tom. "Nice!"

"It's part of the bribe," she continued. "We promised the kids that once we completed the hiking part of the trip, we would treat them to a weekend at Sunriver and then continue on to Disneyland."

I turned and smiled at the kids as the mom regarded them sympathetically.

"I'm afraid we had a wretched time of it last night, with the biting flies and mosquitoes and all," she explained. "No amount of insect repellent—natural or toxic—would deter them, and it made it pretty impossible to sleep."

"But we're nearly finished with the challenging part, right, kids?" It was the dad who now piped up with a peppy bit of encouragement. He turned to Tom and remarked with one eyeball on the two young backpackers-by-default, "They've been real troupers."

The troupers were not buying it and were unable to conceal their misery. Perhaps they were endeavoring to visualize, with every agonizing boot step, the hard-earned reward awaiting them just over the next bug-infested ridge.

A few years back, on a return trip from tent camping near the Redwoods of California, Tom and I treated ourselves to a two-night stay at Sunriver.

Sunriver Resort is a very popular vacation spot located in the desert high country of central Oregon, along the Deschutes River and Cascade Mountains. With plenty of options for lodging, Sunriver serves up a great deal of opportunities for enjoyment including swimming and golfing, as well as fishing, biking, rafting, and all of the usual fun-in-the-sun stuff.

Following the scenic route along the beautiful Rogue River of southwest Oregon, we had made our lonesome way northeast toward Sunriver and—after stopping at the occasional small-town museum (Tom and his whole family are history enthusiasts) and after a couple thousand bathroom breaks (bladder the size of a pea)—arrived at our destination by early evening.

With the exception of our twenty-four-hour mosquito escort with bites that felt more like bee stings, it was a really great place. The following morning, we rented a couple of bikes and did a bit of exploring, keeping an eagle eye out for a very much coveted swimming pool.

And lo and behold, and faster than I could say "I'm itchin' for a bitchin' bikini,"—try not to imagine this—we came upon the most enticing swimming pool of our dreams...more or less.

I looked at Tom, and he looked at me, and with an instinctive mutual understanding, we hurried back to our condo, grabbed our swimming gear—that's what real athletes call it...gear—and returned to find us a nice comfy spot on the lush lawn next to the pool and beneath one of the shade trees. With a couple of beach towels, some cool looking shades, sunscreen, cold drinks, and salty snacks, we had ourselves one awesome desert oasis, more or less.

It was a huge swimming pool, and it was filled with families. But that didn't stop the Tom-inator and me. We got in with the rest of the revelers and reveled. Keep in mind that when one enters a pool filled with families, one can count on being kicked by handstanding aquatic gymnasts, head-butted by human torpedoes, cannon-balled by Chunky, and in general knocked about by various underwater arms and legs. I won't even get into the Marco Polo squads. That is to be expected, but what we didn't expect was, once again, adult swim! I know! Were we lucky or what?

That's right. We had been in the pool only ten minutes or so when the lifeguards blew their whistles and ordered everyone to clear the pool for a safety check. After all children had been accounted for by their parents and the lifeguards switched out for a fresh pair, the new on-duty duo blew their whistles and called out "Adult swim!" or something like that.

Tom and I smiled at each other. *This is too good to be true!* I thought. *Are we, senior citizens considerably past the age of reason, now being granted freedom to swim with the total abandonment of swimming years past?*

We commenced to hasten back toward the pool for some battered-free water frivolity when Tom changed course.

He was eyeballing the big, curvy slide that he had watched the kids fly down earlier.

"Let's go try that out!" he called back to me over his shoulder, heading excitedly toward the slide in a semi-gallop.

At about that time, the lifeguard blew his whistle. "No running!" he shouted to Tom.

Actually, I made that part up. Anyway...

Even though the notion of flying down that big waterslide sounded fun at first, memories of childhood ear and sinus infections, the direct result of diving board and slide acrobatics, along with the fact that I had already gone through my midlife crisis, held me back.

"As thrilling as that looks, Tom, I'm going to leave that death-defying feat up to you," I called back to him.

And so I swam about the pool, free as a dolphin, occasionally looking up to watch a grinning, carefree Tom flying with full momentum down the slide, his bald head bobbing up and down after hitting the water, before he turned and headed right back up the ladder for another go. If I know my husband, he was probably counting how many runs he had made, like he does when he skis, and calculating the approximate velocity of each run.

What was even more entertaining was once adult-swim time had expired—now that he had gotten the hang of it—Tom continued to climb the ladder and take his place in the lineup of kids and teens in a competitive "Oh yeah, just watch this one" atmosphere of camaraderie.

Some kids just never truly grow up. But as Tom always says, "There's nothing wrong with that, is there?"

Alas, all good things must come to an end, and in the blink of a chlorinated eye we were off and running, making our way back to Washington. Meandering north on Highway 97 and just outside of a small town named Shaniko, and while in the midst of pondering the deep issue of loads of laundry that would soon be mine to conquer, I happened to glance out my window to see a dead tree along the road that was loaded with shoes. Thousands of shoes, just hanging there proudly and boldly in all the majesty of their, well, shoe-ness!

I now understand that there are many such trees across America and many different explanations regarding who, when, and why. But as we blew past, all I could think was "Wow! That is so cool!"

I often think about that tree and regret not having turned back to take a photo. It was clear to me that this innovative practice had been conceived by teens, perhaps as a rite of passage, or perhaps just a result of orneriness. Either way, for some reason I liked the idea of adding one's shoes to the collection in the shoe tree, rather like a statement of "I once walked this way," more or less.

As it should happen, months later I spotted the beginnings of a new shoe tree just outside the town of Snohomish, Washington, our closest hub for groceries-r-us, gas-r-us, antiques-r-us, and so forth. At the time, the tree had only a few pairs of shoes hanging in it, but over the next year, the number grew.

One day I approached Tom with a brilliant idea. "Tom, why don't we throw our old tennis shoes into the shoe tree down there outside of Snohomish?"

Tom peered at me over the top of his newspaper. That's right. Tom is one of the few remaining Americans who still gets a newspaper and reads it cover to cover every evening—all eight pages.

"It would be so cool, not to mention daring," I said. "When's the last time we were actually daring?" I asked him. "We could buy some spray paint and do them up really bright so that they stand out. It'll be fun."

Now, before you say anything, I realize that I just related to you a couple of paragraphs ago that I had already been through—and survived—my own midlife crisis. I have a small tattoo of a rose behind my left shoulder to prove it (although my father claimed that it looked more like a wart). But there was just something so very tantalizing about adding my shoes to the collection in the tree. It was like saying, "Yes! I know what you mean. I hear you, bro. I walked this planet, too!"

Just for the record, I've never really called anyone *bro*.

Tom's eyebrows arched when he looked at me with eyes that said, *You've got to be kidding me.* But I had a sneaking suspicion that I did stir his interest.

"I'll paint mine a sparkly ruby red, like Dorothy's slippers, and we can paint yours gold, like those of a superhero." I grinned wildly at him.

A couple of weeks later, I went to the craft store and bought the paints. Then one sunny, somewhat dry afternoon, I went out to the backyard and sprayed my old tennis shoes ruby red. As fate would have it, I didn't have enough paint to cover the shoes completely, but I was too cheap to go buy more.

When Tom came home, I informed him that there was gold paint waiting for him on his workbench in the garage. And frankly, that's where the can of gold spray paint remained for quite some time.

Months went by, and then a year. Finally, after about a year and a half, I came home one day to find Tom's shoes on his workbench, lit up brilliantly with gold paint. What's more, they looked even better than mine!

Our shoes were finally ready for the shoe tree; however, now I was beginning to have second thoughts. While Tom was out in the yard trying to get the hang of throwing his shoes into a tree without missing the target and thus hurling them into oncoming traffic, I was inside debating whether or not this was such a good idea after all.

We're not kids, I reasoned. *This is something that kids do. They started it. It's their "thing."*

I wondered why I would want to go invade their territory. It would be like one of those people you see who dresses way too young for his or her age: an older woman wearing a midriff top and very short skirt or an older man with a chain necklace, tight jeans, and baseball cap facing backward.

Nevertheless, we put our shoes in the trunk of our car and decided that we would throw them into the shoe tree on the night of April 28, our wedding anniversary.

Except that on the planned date, by the time we had come back from dining out, it was dark out.

What if someone came by and, not seeing us because it was so dark, wrecked into us?

What if we missed the tree and threw the shoes onto someone's windshield?

What if the sheriff came by and arrested us for misdemeanor mischief? Vandalism? Trespassing?

What if hesitation killed the cat?

Oh, the doubts were endless.

In the end, we did not throw our magnificently painted shoes into the shoe tree, and we headed home after patting ourselves on the back for doing the sensible thing. After all, we were not kids. We had advanced into maturity, the time of life for wisdom, reflection, and loving kindness. The time for silliness was over.

But you can bet your sweet, knotted shoestrings that kids who throw their shoes into shoe trees are not such sissies.

Now wait just a minute! Wait a doggone minute!

On August 30, 2015, Tom and I finally threw our shoes into the shoe tree, because, as the great Yogi Berra once said, "It ain't over until it's over." More or less.

P.S. In 2010, the shoe tree of Shaniko, Oregon, was destroyed by a fire. See "Shoe Tree Requiem, Shaniko, Oregon," on YouTube.

Made in the USA
Lexington, KY
26 April 2017